Discovery Walks in Worcestershire

Brian Conduit

Published by Sigma Leisure – an imprint of
Sigma Press, 1 South Oak Lane, Wilmslow, Cheshire SK9 6AR, England.

British Library Cataloguing in Publication Data
A CIP record for this book is available from the British Library.

ISBN: 1-85058-706-X

Typesetting and Design by: Sigma Press, Wilmslow, Cheshire.

Cover photographs, clockwise from top left: Elmley Castle; the
Malvern Ridge from the Old Hills; Harvington Village *(Brian Conduit)*

Maps: Jeremy Semmens

Photographs: Brian Conduit

Printed by: MFP Design and Print

Disclaimer: the information in this book is given in good faith and is believed to be correct at the time of publication. No responsibility is accepted by either the author or publisher for errors or omissions, or for any loss or injury howsoever caused. Only you can judge your own fitness, competence and experience.

Preface

As a native of Birmingham, the Worcestershire landscape has been well known to me from an early age. In the days before mass car ownership, many Brummies and their Black Country brethren would take a Midland Red bus out into Worcestershire on fine Sunday afternoons and Bank Holidays in order to go for a stroll on the Lickey or Clent Hills, or along the riverside promenades at Evesham, Worcester and Bewdley, or – a little further afield and somewhat more adventurous – over the slopes of that glorious mini-mountain range of the Malverns.

In many ways Worcestershire remains the quintessential English county. Two of the country's loveliest and best-known rivers – the Severn and Avon – flow through it. It has hills that inspired Sir Edward Elgar and A.E. Housman, both sons of Worcestershire. There are delightful old towns of dignified, brick-built Georgian houses and black and white villages with appealing old inns that look as if they have come straight off a chocolate box cover. Everything about Worcestershire is in moderation. The county is of medium size. Most of its hills hover just below or just above the 1000-foot mark; quite high by Midland and southern standards but modest when compared with the Lake District or Snowdonia. The towns are of moderate size; Worcester itself – the largest – has a population of around 93,500. There are many woodlands scattered throughout the county – some of them remnants of the ancient forests of the Midlands – but all of these are intimate rather than vast. It is much the same with the county's historic buildings. There are no great prehistoric monuments, medieval castles or outstanding monastic sites, though there are the remains of monastic churches at Evesham, Pershore and Great Malvern. It does possess one of the finest cathedrals in the country but Worcester is not as large and imposing as York, Durham or Lincoln. The many stately homes and manor houses are appealing in their modesty – even homeliness – with none of the overwhelming grandeur of say Chatsworth or Blenheim.

Although mostly thought of as a predominantly rural county, it should not be overlooked that the traditional county of Worcestershire – the one that had existed for centuries prior to the local government boundary changes of 1974 – extended northwards to the boundaries of Birmingham and included a sizeable slice of the heavily industrialised Black Country, now lost to the county of West Midlands. Parts of the old county therefore have an industrial heritage, along with the older, more traditional and familiar one.

Worcestershire occupies the very heart of England and at the heart of the county is its grandest building. Worcester Cathedral is known the world over, not least because of its role as the backcloth to what is generally regarded as the finest view from any cricket ground in England. Could there be a more English scene than this: that most English of games being played in the most English of settings, beside one of the country's foremost rivers, and all within sight of the hills that inspired much of the music of England's greatest composer?

Get on the walking boots because this glorious Worcestershire countryside and heritage can only be appreciated fully by exploring the county's extensive network of public footpaths.

Bran Conduit

Contents

The Walks

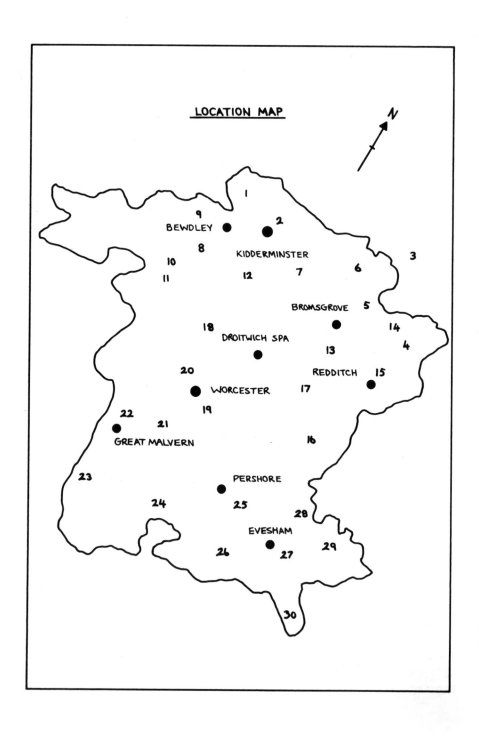

Introduction

In the local government reorganisation of 1974, the ancient county of Worcestershire – the one that had existed since Anglo-Saxon times – suffered two indignities. First it was amalgamated with neighbouring Herefordshire to create a new and wholly artificial county of Hereford and Worcester. Secondly it lost a slice of country in the north – an area of the county that formed part of the Black Country – to the newly created West Midlands. The first problem has been remedied as, in 1998, Hereford and Worcester had a civilised and amicable divorce which has resulted in both regaining their former independence. The loss of the former Worcestershire part of the Black Country remains.

The reason for referring to such political matters at the start of a walking guide is to make clear the precise area covered by this guide. All the thirty walks, with one exception, are within the present county boundaries. The exception – Walk 3 – is just over the boundary within the West Midlands borough of Dudley, included to add to the variety and interest in the selection of routes.

Within these boundaries there is much to discover and enjoy. Worcestershire possesses a great deal of highly attractive and – despite the presence of motorways and the proximity of the West Midlands conurbation – largely unspoilt countryside, a landscape that has inspired, among others, A.E. Housman and Sir Edward Elgar, two of Worcestershire's best-known sons. Much of the terrain is hilly, ideal for walking and perhaps something of a surprise to first time visitors who think of the Midlands as being fairly flat. The county has one major historic city, several attractive small towns and as fine a collection of appealing villages as can be found anywhere in the country, many of them characterised by black and white, half-timbered cottages. In addition, Worcestershire has it fair share of historic monuments and architectural treasures.

The county lies at the very heart of England and because of this central location, the many hilltop vantage points around its perimeter enable walkers to survey quite a huge and varied slice of the country. On the west - from the Malvern and Abberley hills - you look out over the

Welsh border country of Shropshire and Herefordshire towards the distant hills of Wales. To the south - from Bredon Hill - you overlook the Vale of Severn and the Cotswolds and in fact a small segment of the latter hills lies just within the county. On the east, Worcestershire merges almost imperceptibly into Warwickshire's Arden and Shakespeare Country. To the north - and in complete contrast - the views from the Clent and Lickey hills are of the heavily industrialised and urbanised fringes of Birmingham and the Black Country.

In some ways Worcestershire resembles a saucer, with most of the hills around the edge and the flatter terrain in the centre. Bisecting the county and flowing past some of its principal towns is the River Severn, for centuries a major commercial artery. In the past, before the advent of the railways, the riverside towns of Bewdley, Worcester and Upton were thriving inland ports. The Severn has two major tributaries. The Avon is perhaps more closely associated with neighbouring Warwickshire and the bard of Stratford, but the river does flow through a large slice of Worcestershire, meandering through the market gardening country of the Vale of Evesham and past the delightful towns of Pershore and Evesham, as well as a string of pretty villages. The other tributary, the Teme, rises in Shropshire, flows through the west of the county and joins the Severn just downstream from Worcester.

The paths beside these rivers, and their smaller tributaries, provide much pleasant walking. More spectacular are the superb hill walks that can be enjoyed on the main ranges – Clent, Lickey, Cotswold, Malvern and Abberley hills – as well as on smaller and individual hills, such as the Old Hills near Malvern and Bredon Hill near Pershore, the latter an outlier of the Cotswolds.

In medieval times much of Worcestershire comprised thick forest. Although most of this woodland cover has gone – felled over the centuries for settlement, agriculture and to satisfy the needs of the Black Country iron industries – delightful remnants of these ancient forests survive. The largest of these is Wyre Forest, whose tree-clad slopes rise above the Severn valley to the west of Bewdley. Now owned and maintained by the Forestry Commission, it is threaded by paths and tracks. Smaller wooded areas can be found at Kingsford Country Park, in Chaddesley Woods near Kidderminster – one of the few remaining fragments of the once extensive Feckenham Forest – and on the slopes of the Abberley, Clent and Lickey hills. All these areas provide attractive walking, as does the orchard country of the Vale of Evesham. This area inevitably looks its best at blossom time but there are always fine views across the wide expanses of the vale to the Cotswolds and Malverns.

Worcestershire's towns are a pleasure to explore and the selection of routes in this guide includes a wholly urban walk through the historic city of Worcester, passing by the cathedral which is undoubtedly the county's major architectural treasure. Some of the other walks, although predominantly rural, take you through the attractive riverside towns of Evesham and Pershore – both formerly possessing great abbeys – Upton upon Severn and Georgian Bewdley; as well as the elegant Victorian spa town of Great Malvern, which also has a fine priory church, and the canal town of Stourport-on-Severn, the only town in England created as a result of the canals.

The walks also take you through a large proportion of the picture postcard villages for which Worcestershire is renowned. Among the most outstanding of these are Elmley Castle and Great Comberton nestling below Bredon Hill, Cleeve Prior and Harvington in the Vale of Evesham, Ombersley and Upper Arley in the Severn valley, the Cotswold village of Broadway at the foot of steep Fish Hill, Feckenham and Inkberrow in the east of the county and Chaddesley Corbett in the north.

A number of long-distance footpaths cross the county. These are the North Worcestershire Path, Worcestershire Way, Wychavon Way, Severn Way and a short part of the Cotswold Way. Stretches of all these well-waymarked routes are used in the following selection of walks.

However there is more to discovering Worcestershire than just attractive landscapes, old towns and pretty villages. All the routes in this guide have some sort of heritage theme to reveal the different facets of the county's history and development. They take in most of the historic sites – prehistoric forts, abbeys and priories, manor houses, stately homes – and also include stretches of canal towpaths and disused railway tracks, part of the county's industrial heritage.

The guide covers all parts of Worcestershire, a county at the heart of England whose countryside, towns, villages and historic buildings are the very essence of traditional England. The extensive network of public footpaths enables you to explore and enjoy all this and, at the same time, perhaps sample some of the old pubs and tea shops which are also a welcoming feature of the Worcestershire landscape.

General Information

As the walks include many sites of historic interest and you will no doubt wish to visit some of these, it is disappointing if you find them closed. Therefore, it is important to check opening times – which vary considerably. Country houses and some museums are often closed during the winter months and even during the summer, may have very restricted opening times. The nearest Tourist Information Centres will provide you with details, as well as up-to-date information on public transport and hotels, guest houses and bed and breakfast establishments.

Local Tourist Information Centres

Bewdley: 01299 404740

Broadway: 01386 852937

Bromsgrove: 01527 831809

Droitwich Spa: 01905 774312

Evesham: 01386 446944

Kidderminster: 01562 829400

Malvern: 01684 892289

Pershore: 01386 554262

Redditch: 01527 60806

Tenbury Wells: 01584 810136

Upton upon Severn: 01684 594200

Worcester: 01905 726311

Useful Addresses

Heart of England Tourist Board, Woodside, Larkhill Road, Worcester WR5 2EF. Tel:01905 763436

National Trust (Severn Regional Office), Mythe End House, Tewkesbury, Gloucestershire GL20 6EB. Tel:01684 850051

English Heritage, Customer Services, PO Box 9019, London W1A 0JA. Tel:0171 9733434

Woodland Trust, Autumn Park, Grantham, Lincolnshire NG31 6LL. Tel:01476 581111

Countryside Commission, John Dower House, Crescent Place, Cheltenham, Gloucestershire GL50 3RA. Tel:01242 521381

Forestry Commission, Information Department, 231 Corstorphine Road, Edinburgh EH12 7AT. Tel:0131 334 0303

Ramblers' Association, 1/5 Wandsworth Road, London SW8 2XX. Tel:0171 5826878

Acknowledgements

I am grateful for the invaluable assistance – and the many useful leaflets – acquired from the various tourist information centres throughout Worcestershire, and for the help received from Trevor McAvoy and Richard Jones, Senior Rights of Way Officers for Worcestershire County Council.

The Country Code

Please observe this when walking in the countryside.

* Enjoy the countryside and respect its life and work

* Guard against all risk of fire

* Take your litter home

* Fasten all gates

* Help to keep all water clean

* Keep your dogs under control

* Protect wildlife, plants and trees

* Keep to public paths across farmland

* Take special care on country roads

* Leave livestock, crops and machinery alone

* Make no unnecessary noise

* Use gates and stiles to cross fences, hedges and walls

1. Trimpley Reservoir and Eymore Wood

Start/Parking: Upper Arley – grid reference 766802

Distance: 3½ miles (5.6km)

Category: Easy

Refreshments: Harbour Inn and Old Bakehouse Tearoom at Upper Arley, refreshment bar at Arley station

Terrain: Mainly riverside and woodland paths

OS Maps: Landranger 138, Explorer 218

Public Transport: Buses from Kidderminster and Bridgnorth or, for a more scenic and interesting alternative, travel on the steam-hauled Severn Valley Railway from Kidderminster, Bewdley or Bridgnorth and walk down the lane from Arley station to the footbridge over the River Severn

Explore & Discover

The River Severn is followed downstream, mainly along the bottom edge of the steep-sided Eymore Wood, before reaching Trimpley Reservoir. Much of the return leg is through attractive woodland, with extensive views across the Severn valley to the Shropshire hills. Arley is one of the stations on the steam-hauled Severn Valley Railway.

Route Directions

Start on the north side of the footbridge over the River Severn [A] and, facing the river, turn left along a riverside path, part of both the Worcestershire Way and Severn Way. Keep along the attractive, tree-lined riverbank – there are steps and stiles in places – crossing a footbridge over a brook to reach a fork.

Take the right-hand path – keeping on the Severn Way – along the bottom edge of the steeply sloping Eymore Wood, pass under a railway bridge and continue to a stile. Climb it to emerge from the trees, bear slightly left away from the river across a meadow, pass through a narrow belt of trees and continue to a footpath post. Turn left, in 'Reservoir'

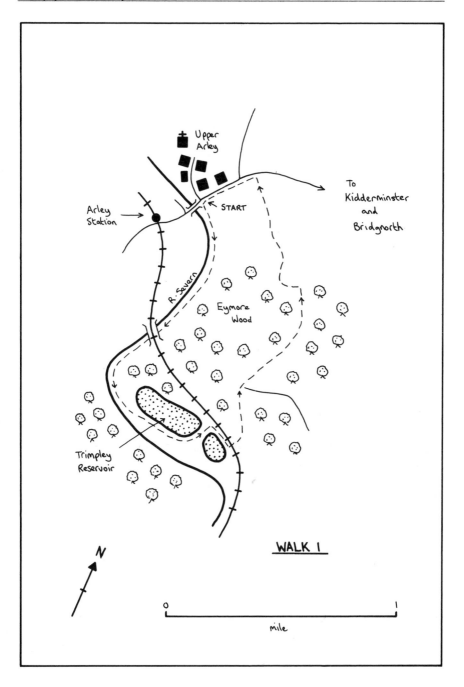

direction, head up an embankment and at the top, bear right alongside Trimpley Reservoir. From this more elevated position, there are grand views over the Severn valley [B].

Follow the curve of the reservoir to the left and in front of a gate and stile, turn right down steps to a tarmac drive and keep ahead, between the lower reservoir on the right and the railway line on the left. At a public footpath sign to Eymore Wood Car Park, turn left to climb a stile, cross the railway line and go through a gate to re-enter Eymore Wood. Follow an uphill path through the trees, take the left-hand path at a fork, bear left on meeting another path and continue steadily uphill to a lane.

Cross over and keep ahead along a winding, undulating track, following a blue-waymarked route. Take care to keep ahead at a sawmill, after which the track starts to descend. After crossing a footbridge over a brook, the track turns left – initially beside the brook – but soon bears right and heads uphill to emerge from the trees. Turn right to continue along a winding, hedge-lined path and now outstanding views open up over the Severn valley, with the top of the tower of Arley church visible in the middle distance. The path eventually descends to a gate. Go through and turn left down a lane into Upper Arley and back to the start.

Upper Arley

Features of Interest

A. From a distance, the small village of Upper Arley makes a picturesque scene, its houses rising steeply above the east bank of the River Severn to the 14th-century church. From the latter, a short building with a stocky west tower, there is a superb view over the valley. On the other side of the river – reached by a footbridge and lane – is Arley station on the Severn Valley Railway. The railway was built in 1858-62 to link Shrewsbury and Worcester and after being closed, was restored and reopened as a private, steam-hauled railway. It operates between Kidderminster and Bridgnorth. If the station looks familiar, it is because its authentic appearance makes it much in demand from film and television crews.

B. The reservoir was constructed in the 1960s to supplement Birmingham's water supply from the Elan Valley in mid-Wales. It has a most attractive location, above the Severn and on the edge of Eymore Wood, and has become a popular recreational amenity for sailors, naturalists, fishermen and walkers.

2. Kingsford Country Park and Cookley

Start/Parking: Kingsford Country Park, Blakeshall Lane car park – grid reference 836822

Distance: 6 miles (9.7km)

Category: Easy

Refreshments: Bulls Head and Eagle at Cookley

Terrain: Field and woodland tracks and paths, with a middle stretch along a canal towpath

OS Maps: Landranger 138, Explorer 219

Public Transport: The walk could be started from Cookley which is served by buses from Kidderminster

Canal near Cookley

Explore & Discover

From the thick woodlands of Kingsford Country Park, the route heads across fields, descending gently into the Stour valley to reach the Staffordshire and Worcestershire Canal. This is followed by a beautiful walk along the towpath to the village of Cookley before returning to the country park. Near the end of the walk comes a short stretch along the wooded escarpment at the south end of Kinver Edge – shared with neighbouring Staffordshire – from which there are the most superb views.

Route Directions

At the car park, take the path to the left of the toilet block, pass beside a barrier – there is a North Worcestershire Path post here – keep along the right edge of a grassy picnic area and pass beside another barrier to a crossroads. Turn left along a path through the trees, keeping parallel to the lane on the left, and pass beside a barrier onto the lane.

Bear right and at a public footpath sign, turn left along a track, passing beside a gate. At a junction of tracks and paths, turn left – following public bridleway and North Worcestershire Path signs – along an enclosed sandy track which eventually emerges, via a gate, onto a lane at a junction. Take the lane ahead and after a quarter of a mile (0.4km), bear left onto an uphill track which curves left and continues to a stile. Climb it, walk along the right field edge, climb another stile and keep ahead across the next field. On the far side, turn right to continue along the left field edge to a stile. Climb it and continue gently downhill along the left edge of the next field. As you descend, there is a fine view ahead over the Stour valley. Climb a stile, keep ahead to the right of farm buildings and after climbing two more stiles, descend steps to a road. Turn left, cross a bridge over the River Stour and in front of a canal bridge, turn right through a fence gap onto the towpath of the Staffordshire and Worcestershire Canal [A].

Turn right beside the tranquil, tree-lined canal and just after passing through Cookley Tunnel, turn sharp right along an uphill, tree-lined path to a road for a brief detour into Cookley village. Turn right into the village and at a fork, take the right-hand road to the church. [B]

Return to the canal towpath, briefly continue along it but immediately after crossing a bridge over an old arm of the canal, turn right over a stile. Turn right onto a track which turns left beside a factory wall, go through a metal gate and keep ahead – re-crossing the Stour – to a T-junction. Turn left along a track which bends right by a farm and keep ahead to a waymarked post. Continue past it along a path which curves right to a metal gate, go through and bear slightly right along a path through a shallow valley to reach a waymarked stile.

After climbing it, keep ahead across grass to continue alongside a wire fence on the left, heading gently uphill. Eventually the path emerges onto a lane via a stile. Bear right, passing side lanes to both right and left, and at a road sign for 'Horses', bear left along a hedge-lined track and pass through a fence gap to re-enter the woodland of Kingsford Country Park [C]. Immediately turn left onto a track which keeps by the left inside edge of the trees to a T-junction and turn right to continue through the woodland.

There are a multitude of tracks and paths through these woods which can be confusing but the route keeps more or less in a straight line to reach the edge of the escarpment. At the next T-junction turn left and at a junction of paths, keep straight ahead gently uphill to emerge onto the edge. The views to the left are magnificent. Continue along a clear and well-surfaced track to a notice board and fingerpost that indicate that this is the starting point for three long-distance footpaths [D].

Turn right here onto the North Worcestershire Path and walk along a gently descending track. Where the North Worcestershire Path turns right, keep straight ahead to return to the start.

Features of Interest

A. The Staffordshire and Worcestershire Canal was designed by the great canal engineer, James Brindley, and opened in 1771. It provided a link between the Trent and Mersey Canal at Great Haywood and the River Severn at Stourport. This stretch of it, between Kinver and Kidderminster, is particularly attractive.

B. The redbrick church at Cookley is Victorian, built in 1849 and enlarged in 1872.

C. Kingsford Country Park, around 200 acres of pine and birch wood, open heathland and sandstone outcrops, is situated in the north of Worcestershire, adjacent to the Staffordshire border. It includes the southern part of the thickly-wooded escarpment of Kinver Edge, a popular destination for local people. From here the extensive views

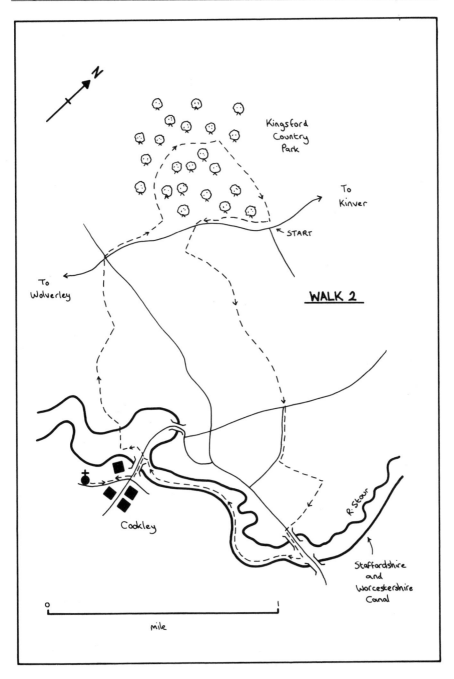

N

Kingsford
Country
Park

To
Kinver

START

To
Wolverley

WALK 2

Cookley

R. Stour

Staffordshire
and
Worcestershire
Canal

0   1

mile

westwards, looking across to Shropshire and the Welsh border, are magnificent.

D. The three long-distance footpaths that start here are the Staffordshire Way, Worcestershire Way and North Worcestershire Path. It is also the county boundary between Worcestershire and Staffordshire.

3. Leasowes Park and Halesowen Abbey

Start/Parking: Leasowes Park, off A458 (Birmingham-Stourbridge road) near the bottom of Mucklow Hill – grid reference 975842

Distance: 4 miles (6.4km)

Category: Easy

Refreshments: Black Horse on A456 just before reaching the ruins of Halesowen Abbey

Terrain: In between the opening and closing stretches along a canal towpath, there is easy and pleasant – if at times muddy – walking across fields and by woodland

OS Maps: Landranger 139, Explorer 219

Public Transport: Buses from Birmingham, Halesowen and Kidderminster

Explore & Discover

Despite being on the fringes of Birmingham and the Black Country and close to the M5 and busy trunk roads, this walk has plenty of pleasant and unspoilt countryside and includes the surprisingly rural oasis of The Leasowes and the secluded – if scanty – remains of Halesowen Abbey. The opening section along the Dudley No.2 Canal is a reminder of the proximity of the Black Country and the industrial heritage of this area, formerly the northern part of Worcestershire but, since the boundary changes of 1974, within the county of West Midlands.

Route Directions

Start by taking the path along the left bank of the canal, signposted 'Manor Way via Canal' [A]. Soon come fine views on both sides: to the right across Halesowen, with the church tower and spire prominent and the Clent Hills beyond, and to the left over Priory Pool and the landscaped parkland of The Leasowes [B]. At the base of steps on the left, turn right to cross the canal and continue along the right bank of the now mostly dried-up and weed-choked canal. On joining a tarmac path, bear left along it to a T-junction, turn right to continue through a children's play area and keep ahead to emerge onto Manor Way.

Turn right and after about 50 yards (46m), cross the road at a crossing point – take care as this is a very busy road – and a little further down the other side, turn left over a stile, at a public footpath sign 'Illey via Abbey Ponds'. Walk along the left edge of a field and over to the right are the ruins of Halesowen Abbey, partly incorporated into farm buildings [C]. Climb a stile, bear slightly left across a field – the banks and hollows are the remains of the earthworks and fish ponds of the abbey – cross a plank footbridge over a brook and keep ahead to a waymarked post. Bear left, continue between the field edge on the right and the brook below on the left and bear right to climb a stile.

Keep along the left edge of the next field and after a few yards, turn left down steps, climb another stile and continue along the left edge of the next two fields, climbing a stile and still with the brook to the left. In the corner of the second field, follow the field edge to the right and head uphill. Near the top, turn left over a stile, immediately turn right, pass through a fence gap and continue along a most attractive, enclosed, tree-lined path. Pass through another fence gap and at the T-junction ahead, turn right along another enclosed path.

The path heads uphill, goes through another fence gap and descends to a stile. The M5 can be both seen and heard over to the left. After climbing the stile, turn right along the right field edge, climb a stile, bear left, head diagonally across the next field and climb another stile. Bear right to a waymarked post, bear right again and head across to the next post on the edge of woodland. Turn left to climb a stile in a hollow, cross a footbridge over a brook, head up a low embankment, bear left and walk across to a stile. Climb it, continue along an enclosed track, turn left over a stile and turn right along the right edge of a sports ground, used by Bartley Green Football Club. Turn right along a track, pass beside a gate onto another track by Illey Hall Farm and turn left.

Turn right over a stile, descend two steps, walk along the right edge of a field and climb a stile in the field corner. Keep along the right edge of the next field but after about 100 yards (91m), turn right over a stile and turn left to continue along the top edge of a sloping field. The path bears right to cut across the field corner, rejoins the hedge on the left and shortly bears right again across the field to cross a brook. Keep ahead along a farm track towards the abbey ruins, ignore the first stile on the right but just after a footpath post, bear right to follow the

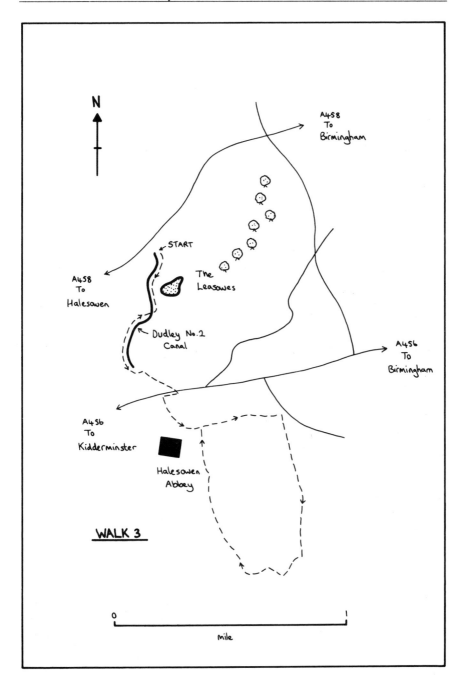

N

A458
To
Birmingham

START

The
Leasowes

A458
To
Halesowen

Dudley No.2
Canal

A456
To
Birmingham

A456
To
Kidderminster

Halesowen
Abbey

WALK 3

0   1

mile

hedgeline to a stile almost hidden in a slight dip. Climb it, keep straight ahead across a field and climb another stile on the far side. Turn left, here rejoining the outward route, and retrace your steps to the start.

Dudley No. 1 Canal, Leasowes Park

Features of Interest

A. Dudley No.2 Canal, opened in 1798, was constructed to provide a link between Dudley No.1 Canal and the Worcester and Birmingham Canal at Selly Oak. Much of it has been filled in but this stretch is managed by the Lapal Canal Trust.

B. The Leasowes Park has tremendous landscape and historic value, especially being located on the edge of a heavily urbanised and industrialised area. It was the home of the 18th-century poet William Shenstone, who enhanced it to look as picturesque as possible, creating areas of woodland, grassy glades, cascades and a pool. He even constructed the mock ruins of a medieval priory. It was one of the first natural landscape gardens in England and was much visited at the time but fell into disrepair after Shenstone's death in 1763. It is currently being restored to something like its former glory by Dudley Council.

C. Little survives of Halesowen Abbey, a Premonstratensian monastery founded by King John in 1214, but the site is an interesting one because of the considerable earthworks and the locations of the monastic fishponds that can be traced in the vicinity of the remains. Some of the ruins are incorporated into the nearby farm and the most complete surviving building is the infirmary. The abbey was dissolved by Henry VIII in 1538. Public access is restricted to weekends only during July and August.

4. Wythall Church and Icknield Street

Start/Parking: Forhill Picnic Place, off road between Drakes Cross and West Heath – grid reference 055755

Distance: 4 miles (6.4km)

Category: Easy

Refreshments: Peacock at start, Coach and Horses at bottom of Weatheroak Hill

Terrain: Gently undulating route mainly on field paths, with a fairly steep climb along a narrow lane at the end

OS Maps: Landranger 139, Explorer 220

Public Transport: The walk could be started from Wythall church which is served by buses from Birmingham and Redditch

Explore & Discover

Field paths – including part of the North Worcestershire Path – are followed to the adjacent Wythall church and Midland Transport Museum. After a descent of Weatheroak Hill, the last part of the route is a climb along a narrow and sunken lane which is on the line of the old Roman road of Icknield Street.

Route Directions

With your back to the toilet block, head across the grass to the far end of the picnic site, descend steps and climb a stile onto a road. Turn right and at a North Worcestershire Path post, turn left through a belt of trees to a stile.

Climb it, bear slightly right across a field, making for a waymarked post on the far side, and bear left through a fence gap. Walk along the left edge of the next two fields and in the corner of the second field, keep ahead to cross a footbridge over a brook. Turn right over a stile, pass to the right of old farm buildings, continue along a left field edge, above a moat on the left, and climb a stile in the field corner.

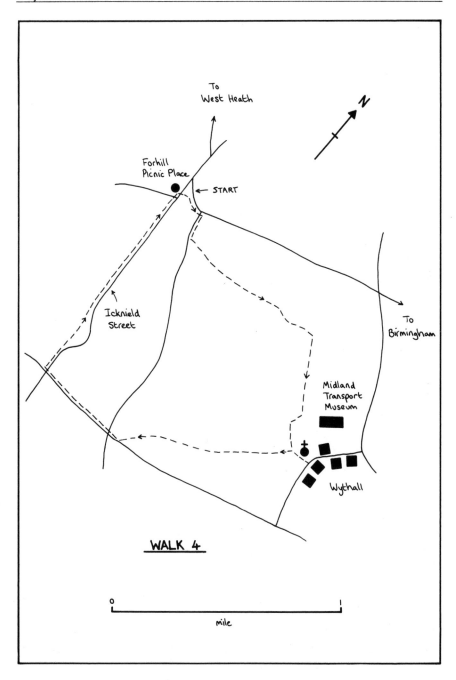

WALK 4

Turn left along the left edge of a golf course, follow the edge round to the right – the route is well-waymarked – and look out for where you continue along a tree-lined path. The path meanders along the edge of the course, continues alongside the high boundary fence of the Britannic Assurance Company complex and finally bears right across a corner of the course to a stile. Climb it, turn left along the left edge of a field, follow the edge to the right and keep along it to a T-junction of paths. Turn left to a gate in the field corner, go through and walk along a farm track to a road. Wythall church [A] is just to the left and where the road bends right by the church, keep ahead to visit the Midland Museum of Transport [B]. Return to the gate in the field corner and after going through it again, bear left and walk diagonally across the field, making for a hedge gap on the far side to the right of a pool where there is a waymarked post. Go through the gap, bear slightly right across the next field and head downhill, aiming for the middle of the line of trees in front. On the far side, look out for where a path leads to a footbridge over a brook and after crossing it, keep along the right field edge. Climb a stile, head gently uphill along the right edge of the next field, climb another stile in the top corner and bear slightly left across a field. Climb a stile in a fence and continue in the same direction to climb another stile in the far corner onto a road.

Turn right and keep ahead at a crossroads along Weatheroak Hill which descends to another crossroads at the bottom by the Coach and Horses pub. Turn right – in the Forhill direction – along a narrow lane which is on the line of the Roman Icknield Street [C]. Where this lane bears slightly right after crossing a stream, keep ahead over a stile and continue uphill along the left edge of a field. Bear right in the field corner, go through a gate to rejoin the lane and follow it uphill back to the start.

Features of Interest

A. This imposing Victorian church, built in 1862, is sadly now derelict and has to be viewed from the road. The tall brick saddleback tower was added in 1903.

B. The full title is the Birmingham and Midland Museum of Transport. Although mainly a bus museum, it does have some old fire engines and battery-operated electric vehicles. There is also a miniature railway around the grounds. The museum is generally open at week-ends only from Easter to the beginning of November.

C. Icknield – or Ryknild – Street was a Roman road that ran across the Midlands from Derbyshire to Gloucestershire. Northwards from here, the line of it passes through some of the suburbs of Birmingham.

5. Waseley Hills and Frankley

Start/Parking: Waseley Hills Country Park, North Car Park — grid reference 973783

Distance: 8 miles (12.9km)

Category: Moderate

Refreshments: Café at Visitor Centre, Black Horse at Illey

Terrain: Several fairly modest ascents and descents; some of the field paths are likely to be muddy at times

OS Maps: Landranger 139, Explorer 219

Public Transport: None

Explore & Discover

Although sandwiched between the south-western suburbs of Birmingham and the edge of the Black Country and bisected by the M5 motorway, this is a surprisingly rural walk with some fine wooded stretches and impressive views, especially from the toposcope on Windmill Hill near the start. Apart from Windmill Hill, the chief focal points are the hilltop landmark of Frankley Beeches, the isolated Frankley church, Bartley Reservoir and the hamlet of Illey.

Route Directions

It is worthwhile to begin by making a brief detour to the top of Windmill Hill for the view. Facing the Visitor Centre, pass to the left of it to a footpath post, go through a kissing gate in a fence and head uphill, in the Lickey Hills direction. After negotiating a minor embankment, make for the toposcope at the top of Windmill Hill [A]. The contrasting views from here take in the southern suburbs of Birmingham, the Lickey Hills and a large slice of rural Worcestershire.

Retrace your steps down to the front of the Visitor Centre and turn right along a track that leads off from the far end of the car park. After going through a kissing gate, the track bends left and later keeps parallel to a road on the left. Look out for a footbridge over a ditch on the left, cross

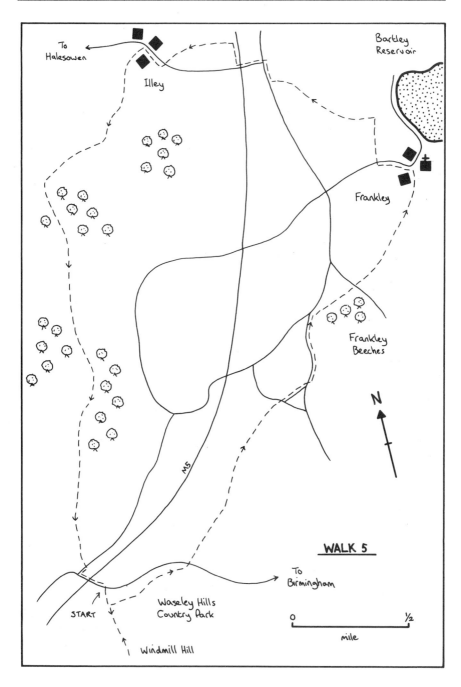

To Halesowen

Bartley Reservoir

Illey

Frankley

Frankley Beeches

N

WALK 5

M5

To Birmingham

START

Waseley Hills Country Park

Windmill Hill

0   ½

mile

it and keep ahead to the road. Cross over and, at a public footpath sign, take the track opposite to Gannow Green Farm. Where the track turns left, keep ahead along a tree-lined track – it later narrows to a path – heading through trees across the top of an embankment and descending to reach a tarmac track. To the right is a housing estate on the edge of Birmingham. Turn left along the track but after a few yards, bear left onto a path that continues once more across the top of an embankment, parallel to a hedge on the left, and descends to a track in front of a bridge.

Cross the bridge – it goes over a disused railway track – climb a metal fence and head across a field to climb a stile in the far right corner. Continue slightly uphill across the next field, climb a stile onto a lane, turn right and in front of a farm, bear left to a T-junction. Turn left along a road and after nearly half a mile (0.8km), bear right onto a track and continue along the right edge of a field up to Frankley Beeches. In the field corner, take the path ahead through the trees to emerge onto a road [B].

Cross over, climb a metal fence and head downhill along the left edge of a field. The large expanse of water seen ahead is Bartley Reservoir [C]. Go through a gate in the field corner and continue along an en-

Frankley church

closed path – later a track – to Frankley church [D]. Turn left along a lane and where it starts to bear left, turn right over a stile. Walk straight across a field – there are now particularly fine views of the reservoir – and look out for a rather unclear and half-hidden stile in the hedge on the far side. Climb it, turn left and follow the field edge as it bears right. In the corner, climb a metal stile and keep ahead along an enclosed tarmac path by garden fences on the right. At a fork, take the left-hand path, keeping by a hedge on the left, which curves right to a T-junction. Turn left, climb another metal stile and walk along the right edge of a field, by iron railings on the right. At the corner of these railings, bear slightly left and continue across the field to climb a stile onto a road.

Keep ahead to another road, turn right and take the first turning on the left – signposted to Halesowen – to cross the M5. Immediately turn right over a stile, walk along the right edge of a field, parallel to the motorway, and in the corner – where you briefly join a track – turn left over another stile. As you head across a field making for a hedge gap on the far side, fine views open up of Halesowen church, the Clent Hills and the edge of the Black Country. Go through the gap, continue along the right edge of a field, go through another wide gap and keep ahead across the next field, joining and keeping along its right edge to a stile.

Climb it, descend to a lane and turn right into Illey. In front of the Black Horse car park, turn left along a track, at a public footpath sign to Romsley and Waseley, which winds downhill to reach a stile. Climb it, pass in front of a farm, climb another stile and bear right to cross a plank footbridge over a brook. Bear right again across a field, passing to the right of a small circular pond, climb a stile to the left of a gate and continue across the next field. On the far side, descend steps into trees, turn right to cross a footbridge over a brook, climb a stile and turn left along the left field edge. Follow the edge to the right, at a footpath post turn left over a stile – joining the well-waymarked Illey Way – and head across a field, making for a waymarked post on the far side on the edge of woodland. Continue through Twiland Wood, descend steps to cross a footbridge over a brook, climb steps on the other side and at the top, follow a path to the right. Continue through the wood, exit via a stile and walk along the left edge of the trees, looking out for a stile on the right.

Climb it, keep in the same direction along the edge of the wood and after a crossroads, continue along the left inside edge of the trees. Head uphill to emerge from the wood via a stile.

Now keep along the right edge of woodland, climb a stile and continue along the left edge of a field. After climbing two stiles in quick succession, head across the corner of the next field and continue steadily uphill along its left edge to a stile. Climb it, keep along the left edge of the next field and climb a stile onto a road. Turn right to a T-junction, turn left to recross the M5 and take the first turning on the right to return to the Country Park.

Features of Interest

A. Waseley Hills Country Park comprises 150 acres of open hillside and small areas of woodland on the south-western fringes of Birmingham. The toposcope on Windmill Hill points out the many and varied places that can be seen in clear conditions from this superb vantage point.

B. This abrupt hilltop viewpoint, 829 feet (256m) high and crowned by a fine stand of beeches, was given to the National Trust by the Cabdury family – whose chocolate factory at Bournville is nearby – in 1930.

C. Bartley Reservoir, opened in 1937, is a storage reservoir for the city of Birmingham. The water is piped from a series of catchment reservoirs in the Elan and Claerwen valleys in mid-Wales.

D. Despite the proximity of the housing estates and high-rise flats on the edge of Birmingham, this small and much restored medieval church still retains a secluded and rural atmosphere. The short tower was added in 1751.

6. Clent Hills and Uffmoor Wood

Start/Parking: Clent Hills Country Park, Nimmings Visitor Centre – grid reference 938807

Distance: 6½ miles (10.5km)

Category: Moderate

Refreshments: Refreshment kiosk at Visitor Centre, Hill Tavern at base of Adam's Hill

Terrain: Two moderate ascents and descents followed by fairly flat field and woodland walking

OS Maps: Landranger 139, Explorer 219

Public Transport: The walk can be started from Clent village which is served by an infrequent bus service between Kidderminster and Hagley

Explore & Discover

The views from this walk could hardly be more contrasting: across the highly urbanised and industrialised area of Birmingham and the Black Country in one direction, and over a wide swathe of the rural Midlands to the outline of the distant Wrekin and the Clee, Abberley and Malvern hills in the other direction. The Clent Hills, now in the care of the National Trust, have long been a favourite recreational area for the people of Birmingham and the Black Country. The route goes over two of the hills – Adam's and Walton – includes the highest point (1035 feet, 315m) high, and also passes through a beautiful area of ancient woodland. Historic interest is provided by the Four Stones on the summit of Adam's Hill and two fine old churches.

Route Directions

Facing the Visitor Centre, turn left up steps, cross one track and turn right along the second track. The track winds uphill almost imperceptibly to reach a viewing platform just below the summit of Adam's Hill. The superb and extensive views from here take in the Black Country, the Wrekin and the Clee, Abberley and Malvern hills. Below the mock ruins of 'Hagley Castle' can be seen, one of a number of 18th-century follies that adorn the grounds of Hagley Hall. A brief detour along the broad track to the left leads up to the Four Stones at the top of Adam's Hill, 997 feet (304m) high and an even more magnificent viewpoint [A].

From here retrace your steps and continue along the broad ridge, descending steadily all the while and enjoying the grand views all around. When you see buildings below on the right, a short detour along a track leads to the Hill Tavern. Eventually you reach a T-junction. Turn left, pass beside a barrier, continue downhill along a tarmac drive to a lane and turn left to follow this winding lane into Clent village.

At a crossroads in front of the church, [B] keep ahead for a few yards and then bear left, at a public footpath sign, along a path enclosed between a hedge on the right and the church wall on the left. Go through a kissing gate, take the uphill path ahead across a field, pass through a gap in a line of trees and continue uphill to go through a kissing gate at the far, narrow end of the field. Keep ahead through woodland, at a fork take the right-hand path – this is a bridleway – to pass a National Trust 'Clent Hills' sign and continue along the right inside edge of the trees. Keep ahead at the next public bridleway sign and the path continues to rise, eventually emerging into open country. At a waymarked post, follow the main (broadest) path which bears slightly left across the gorse-strewn hilltop to reach the trig point on the summit of Walton Hill, at 1035 feet (315m) the highest point on the Clent Hills and another superb viewpoint.

From here take the path which leads off the main track to the right of the trig point – there is a footpath post – and descends through trees to a tarmac track. Turn left and at a T-junction, turn right along a lane. At the next T-junction, turn left and then immediately right at a public footpath sign, climb a stile and walk along the right edge of two fields, passing through a hedge gap. Frankley Beeches can be seen straight ahead. About 100 yards (91m) before reaching the corner of the second field, turn left onto a path that heads across to a stile, climb it and continue in the same direction across the next field to climb a stile in the corner onto a lane.

Turn right, almost immediately turn left over a stile, turn half-right and walk across a field to climb a stile on the far side. Keep along the right edge of the next field, climb another stile and immediately turn left to continue gently downhill along the left edge of the next two fields towards Uffmoor Wood, climbing a stile. In the far corner of the second

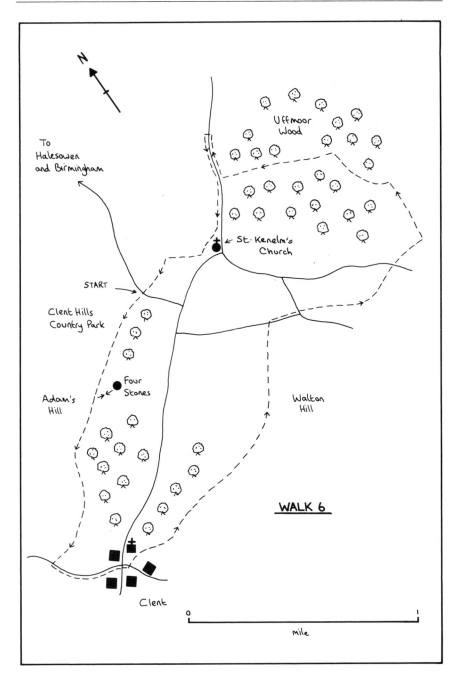

N

To
Halesowen
and Birmingham

Uffmoor
Wood

St. Kenelm's
Church

START

Clent Hills
Country Park

Adam's
Hill

Four
Stones

Walton
Hill

WALK 6

Clent

0   1

mile

field, turn left down steps and climb the stile ahead – not the yellow-waymarked stile to the right – to enter Uffmoor Wood [C].

Descend steps, cross a footbridge, ascend steps on the other side, cross another footbridge and follow a path to a T-junction. Turn left and about 50 yards (46m) in front of a fence, turn right along a broad, straight track. At the next T-junction, turn left along another straight track, eventually passing beside a barrier into the Woodland Trust car park. Before emerging onto a lane, turn right beside another barrier and follow a path through the wood, keeping parallel with the lane. At a T-junction, turn left and go through a gate onto the lane.

Cross over, take the track opposite and at a public footpath sign, turn left through a gate. Continue first along an enclosed path, then through woodland and then along the left edge of a field, heading steadily uphill all the while towards St Kenelm's church and climbing a series of stiles. Another section of enclosed path leads to one more stile and after climbing that, keep ahead, passing to the right of the spring that is said to mark the site of St Kenelm's martyrdom.

Climb steps and go through a gate into the churchyard, passing to the right of the church [D]. Keep ahead along a tarmac path for about 20 yards and then bear right – near some large yew trees – across the churchyard to climb a stile. Bear slightly left across a field, pass through a line of trees, at a waymarked post, and keep in the same direction across the next field to a stile. After climbing it, turn left along a gently ascending track and at a fork, take the right-hand track to continue uphill across grassy slopes to a stile. Climb it onto a lane opposite the car park.

Features of Interest

A. Although they may look like Worcestershire's equivalent of Stonehenge, the Four Stones were erected here in the 18th century by the poet William Shenstone, who lived just down the road at The Leasowes, (See Walk 4) in order to make a picturesque scene.

B. Apart from the 15th-century chancel and west tower, Clent church was mostly rebuilt in the 19th century.

C. This is an ancient woodland, one of several in Worcestershire once owned by a local brush making company in order to have a constant supply of timber for brush handles. There is a mixture of new conifer

The Four Stones, Adam's Hill

plantings, mainly larch and pine, and some older broadleaved trees. The wood is now owned and maintained by the Woodland Trust for public enjoyment and recreation.

D. As you walk up towards this delightful little sandstone church, steps on the left lead down to the spring that marks the spot where, according to legend, Kenelm, a 9th-century boy prince of Mercia was murdered and buried. Although heavily restored in the 19th century, St Kenelm's church retains much of its original Norman work in the nave and chancel and has a south porch dating from the Tudor period. Originally an outlying chapel of Halesowen, it became the parish church for nearby Romsley in 1841. Despite the visible proximity of the Black Country, this peaceful churchyard and small church have an air of tranquillity normally only found in the remoter northern and western parts of the country.

7. Chaddesley Woods and Harvington Hall

Start: Chaddesley Corbett, by the church – grid reference 893736

Distance: The full walk is 8½ miles (13.7km); the shorter version which omits the extension to Harvington Hall is 5½ miles (8.9km)

Category: Moderate

Parking: Roadside parking at Chaddesley Corbett

Refreshments: Swan and Talbot pubs plus tearoom at Chaddesley Corbett, café at Harvington Hall

Terrain: Well-waymarked route mainly along field and woodland tracks and paths

OS Maps: Landranger 139, Explorer 219

Public Transport: Buses from Kidderminster and Bromsgrove

Explore & Discover

This figure of eight walk is based on the attractive village of Chaddesley Corbett. The shorter version of the walk takes you on a circular route across fields to the east of the village to the lovely Chaddesley Woods, remnants – though reasonably sizeable ones – of the medieval Forest of Feckenham. On the full walk, you head across fields to the west of Chaddesley Corbett to the moated manor house of Harvington Hall, well worth the extra mileage, especially as it is across almost entirely flat terrain.

Route Directions

With your back to the church, turn left through the village [A] and opposite the Swan Inn, turn right along a track. At a fork, take the left-hand track, climb a stile onto a tarmac drive and keep ahead along a hedge-lined track.

The track later keeps along the left edge of a field to a stile. Climb it, head uphill across the next two fields, climbing a stile, and on the far side of the second field, climb another stile to enter Chaddesley Woods

Harvington Hall

[B]. Follow a path through this most attractive woodland, bear right on meeting another path and continue uphill to a T-junction. Turn left onto a clear path but after about 50 yards (46m), bear right onto a narrower path. This junction is not easy to spot but the path continues through the wood, passing two yellow-waymarked posts, to a stile. After climbing it, continue along the right edge of the wood, descending gently to climb a stile in the field corner onto a lane.

Take the path opposite along the right inside edge of the trees. This path – which may be overgrown in places – heads gently uphill and continues to a stile. Climb it and keep ahead along a tarmac track which descends to a lane. Turn left and at a public bridleway sign, turn right through a gate. Walk along an enclosed path to re-enter woodland and continue to a gate. Go through, keep ahead along an enclosed path to go through another and after going through one more gate, continue along a track, passing to the right of a cottage.

The track bends right to keep along the left edge of a narrow grassy strip, between woodland both sides, to a metal gate. Go through, continue along a tree-lined track to a T-junction and turn right to a lane. Turn right, ignore the first public footpath sign on the left but at the second one – where the lane forks – turn left over a stile and walk across a field to a stile on the far side.

After climbing it, continue along the right edge of a tree nursery, climb a stile and keep ahead across rough grass to join a concrete track. Go through a waymarked metal gate into a farmyard, climb a stile and keep ahead along a track to a waymarked post where you turn right to cross a ditch. Bear left diagonally across a field to a stile, climb it and turn left along the left field edge, passing through an avenue of trees. Climb another stile, continue along the right field edge, climb a stile in the corner and keep ahead to a T-junction.

Turn left and look out for a yellow-waymarked post where you turn right to cross a plank footbridge. Walk along a narrow path, between a wire fence on the left and the edge of Chaddesley Woods on the right, climb a stile at the corner of the wood and keep ahead along a fence-lined path to another stile. Climb it, head straight across the next field and on the far side, cross a tarmac drive and continue along the left field edge. To the right is a view of the Clent Hills and as the path descends, an impressive view appears ahead, looking across a pool to Chaddesley Corbett church.

Climb a stile in the field corner, walk along the left edge of the next field, climb a stile and continue by the pool to climb another one. Turn right along the right field edge, follow the edge to the left and at a hedge corner, turn right to continue along the right field edge and pass through a hedge gap onto a track. Turn left, here picking up the outward route, and retrace your steps to Chaddesley Corbett.

For the extension to Harvington Hall, turn right on emerging onto the village street and take the first lane on the left. At a public footpath sign, turn left along a hedge-lined track and in front of a gate and stile, turn right through a hedge gap and head straight across a field, going over a slight brow. Continue downhill along the right edge of the next field, go through a gate, keep along the right field edge but look out for a yellow-waymarked stile on the right.

After climbing it, turn left along the left field edge, turn left through a hedge gap in the corner, immediately turn right through another and turn left along a track. The track turns right and at the next field corner, keep ahead along a track which bends left and passes beside a gate onto a lane at a bend. Turn left and follow the lane to the entrance to Harvington Hall and the Catholic church [C]. From here retrace your

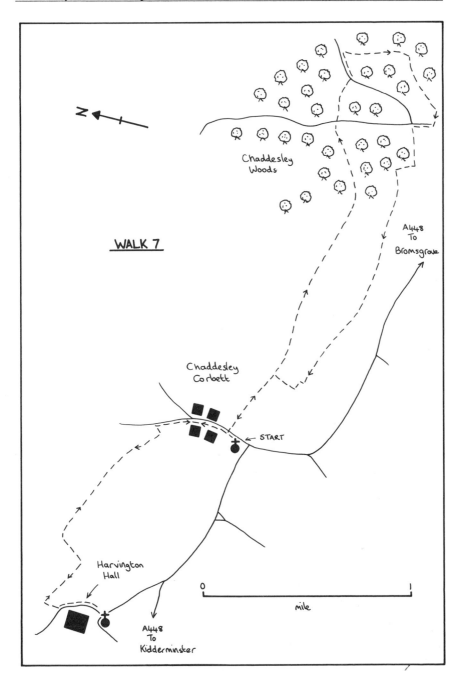

WALK 7

Chaddesley
Woods

Chaddesley
Corbett

A448
To
Bromsgrove

START

Harvington
Hall

A448
To
Kidderminster

0

mile

steps to the start and on the final stretch, you enjoy some fine views of Chaddesley Corbett church, with the woods on the horizon.

Features of Interest

A. The main street at Chaddesley Corbett is exceptionally attractive, with handsome brick-built houses, old inns and a number of black and white cottages. At its southern end is the church, whose soaring tower and spire – rebuilt in 1778 after its medieval predecessor had become unsafe – is a prominent local landmark. The church is particularly interesting. It dates back to the 12th century and has some impressive Norman arches in the nave and a superb 14th-century chancel. It is also unusual in being dedicated to the little known St Cassian.

B. In the Middle Ages, the royal hunting ground of Feckenham Forest occupied much of Worcestershire and the delightful collection of woodlands that make up Chaddesley Woods are the largest surviving remnants. (See Walk 16 for details on Feckenham Forest)

C. With its moat, mellowed stone and brickwork, uneven floors and all kinds of nooks and crannies, Harvington Hall is everyones' idea of what the perfect Elizabethan manor house should look like. Although there is some earlier medieval work, most of the house was built in the 1580s by Humphrey Pakington and many of the rooms still have their original Elizabethan wall paintings. The Pakingtons were a Catholic family and as this was a time of widespread anti-Catholic persecution, the house contains a large number of priest holes, hiding places to enable the priests to avoid detection by the authorities. After becoming derelict in the 19th century, the house was purchased for the Roman Catholic archdiocese of Birmingham in 1923 which subsequently restored it. The nearby Catholic church was built in 1825.

---

8. Ribbesford and Bewdley

Start/Parking: Blackstone Meadows Country Park, off B4194 (Bewdley-Stourport road) – grid reference 792743

Distance: 2½ miles (4km)

Category: Easy

Refreshments: Pubs and cafés at Bewdley

Terrain: Field tracks and paths, second half of route is along a riverside path

OS Maps: Landranger 138, Explorer 218

Public Transport: The walk could be started from Bewdley which is served by buses from Birmingham, Kidderminster and Ludlow, and by the Severn Valley Railway from Kidderminster and Bridgnorth

---

Explore & Discover

After passing the isolated Ribbesford church, the route follows the Worcestershire Way into Bewdley. Leave plenty of time to explore this delightful town, with its fine Georgian houses and quaysides, before taking the riverside path back to the start.

Route Directions

From the far end of the car park, take the path ahead which runs below the A456 embankment on the left down to the River Severn. Turn right onto a riverside path and Blackstone Rock can be seen rearing above the opposite bank. The path follows the curve of the river to the right to emerge onto a road.

Turn left and turn right along the tree-lined drive to Ribbesford church [A]. Turn right in front of the church and walk along a track, signposted Worcestershire Way North, which passes under the A456 and continues to a lane. Cross over, go through a kissing gate and walk along a pleasant, gently descending, enclosed track which narrows to a path and continues towards the houses of Bewdley. Go through another kissing gate, keep ahead along a tree-lined path and about 100 yards (91m) after crossing a plank footbridge, turn right, at a Worcestershire

Way sign, along an enclosed path to emerge onto a narrow street (High Street) in Bewdley.

A short distance to the right – on the corner of Lax Lane – is the fine Georgian house in which Stanley Baldwin, three times Prime Minister, was born in 1867. The route continues to the left along this most attractive street of dignified, brick Georgian houses – both modest and imposing – to a road junction in front of Bewdley church [B]. Turn right down to the bridge, passing the Guildhall on the right, and on the approach to the bridge, bear left along a path to the river.

Turn right to pass under the bridge and continue along Severn Side South. From here, keep beside the river back to the start, initially along a road and later along a riverside path. After passing under a new road bridge, turn right to retrace your steps to the start.

Features of Interest

A. The church, with its distinctive timber bell turret, stands in an isolated position on the edge of Ribbesford Woods above the Severn. Following a lightning strike, most of it was rebuilt in 1877 but some of the older work survives and it remains an intriguing and attractive mixture of Norman, late medieval and Victorian architecture.

B. Bewdley ranks as one of the best preserved and most complete Georgian towns in England. It grew up at an ancient crossing over the River Severn and later developed into an important inland port. The town reached its height in the 18th century but declined after its river traffic was lost, first to the Staffordshire and Worcestershire Canal, which entered the Severn a few miles downstream at Stourport, and later through the coming of the railways. The church, built in 1745-48, stands in the centre of the town at the junction of High Street and Load Street and the latter leads down to Telford's graceful late 18th-century bridge over the Severn. On the way you pass the facade of the Guildhall, built in 1808 and now the Tourist Information Centre. Behind this in the 18th-century Shambles is the Bewdley Museum. The fine Georgian houses that line the former quays of Severn Side North and Severn Side South, either side of the bridge, are reminders of the pre-railway era when many inland riverside towns like Bewdley were bustling centres of trade and commerce.

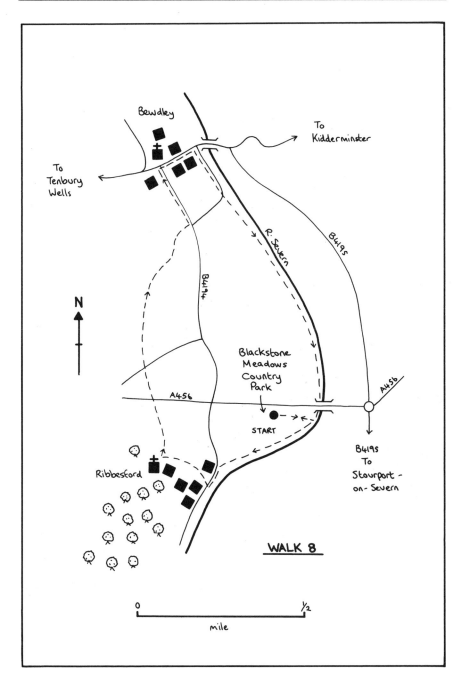

WALK 8

```
┌─────────────────────────────────────────────────────────┐
│                                                         │
│                  9. Wyre Forest                         │
│                                                         │
└─────────────────────────────────────────────────────────┘
```

Start/Parking: Wyre Forest Visitor Centre, off A4117 (Bewdley-Cleobury Mortimer road) – grid reference 752741

Distance: 5 miles (8km)

Category: Easy

Refreshments: Café at Visitor Centre

Terrain: Well-waymarked forest paths and tracks

OS Maps: Landranger 138, Explorer 218

Public Transport: Buses from Birmingham, Kidderminster, Bewdley and Ludlow

Explore & Discover

This walk takes you through some of the finest remaining woodlands of Wyre Forest, one of the more extensive survivals of the ancient forests that once covered much of the Midlands. From the Visitor Centre, you descend into the delightful valley of Dowles Brook, keep beside the brook for about 1 mile (1.6km) and then climb steadily back to the start. There are some grand views over the wooded slopes from the higher points.

Route Directions

Facing the Visitor Centre, [A] take the track that passes to the right of it, initially following a red-waymarked forest trail. Head gently downhill into a dip and at a crossroads, turn left onto an uphill path and follow it to a T-junction.

Turn right along a track and follow it through a lovely part of the forest (New Parks), heading steadily downhill into the valley of Dowles Brook and ignoring all side paths and tracks. The track is a public bridleway and there are blue arrows on posts at regular intervals. Near the bottom the track bends right and at a 'Footbridge' sign, bear left off it and continue along a path to cross a footbridge over Dowles Brook. Keep ahead to a T-junction, turn right to regain the track and continue

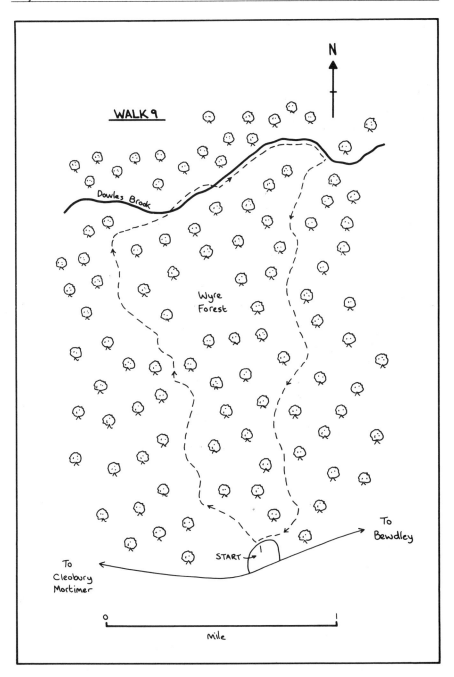

through the valley [B]. Cross a tributary brook to a T-junction, turn right and walk along a path, with the brook on the right. Recross Dowles Brook and continue along the right bank, sometimes above and sometimes beside the brook, as far as a fork.

Here take the right-hand upper path which bends left to a broad straight track which was previously crossed on the descent. This is a disused railway line that once ran through the valley. Cross it and keep ahead along a track which curves right to a junction. Turn left and follow a winding but clear track – it may be muddy in places as it is part of a Horse Trail – through another delightful part of the forest (Shelf Held Coppice). The track keeps above a valley on the left all the while to reach a T-junction.

Turn left – here picking up the red-waymarked route again – and continue steadily uphill. Eventually the track bends right and shortly afterwards, look out for a waymarked post which indicates a turn to the right along a path through conifers. Finally take the left-hand path at a fork to return to the Visitor Centre.

Features of Interest

A. Wyre Forest gives its name to Worcestershire (Wyre-castra) and its thickly wooded slopes rise above the Severn valley to the north and west of Bewdley. It was originally a royal hunting ground and, at its greatest, reached southwards almost to Worcester and extended into Shropshire. Like many of the ancient forests of the Midlands, its timber was greatly prized by the local ironmasters of the Black Country and over the centuries much of the forest was felled. Nowadays Wyre Forest is managed by the Forestry Commission and comprises an attractive mixture of broadleaved and coniferous trees – chiefly oak, beech, birch, Douglas fir, Corsican pine and larch. There are a number of waymarked trails and miles of other paths and tracks through which visitors are free to wander.

B. Dowles Brook flows eastwards through the heart of the forest to join the River Severn just to the north of Bewdley. Evidence of previous industrial activity in this beautiful valley can be seen in the former mill buildings and the disused railway track. The latter, mainly a passenger line, linked Tenbury Wells with Kidderminster.

10. Abberley Village and Hill

Start/Parking: Great Witley, Village Hall car park – grid reference 757657

Distance: 5 miles (8km)

Category: Fairly strenuous

Refreshments: Hundred House Hotel at Great Witley, Manor Arms at Abberley Village

Terrain: Hilly and well-wooded country, with one steep climb and descent

OS Maps: Landranger 150, Explorer 204

Public transport: None

Explore & Discover

The Abberley Hills are a small range of well-wooded hills that rise to over 900 feet (274m) between the Severn and Teme valleys and provide a series of extensive views across the wide valleys to the surrounding hills. The walk passes an ornate Victorian Clock Tower and takes you through the small Abberley village, with its partially ruined Norman church and 19th-century successor. From the village you climb steeply to the highest point on the hills – Abberley Hill itself – and this is followed by a splendid ridge walk before the final descent.

Route Directions

Turn right out of the car park and walk along the road as far as a T-junction in front of the Hundred House Hotel. Turn left and, just after passing a road on the left to Bromyard, take a track on the left at the side of a cottage. After climbing a stile, the track curves steadily uphill through woodland, turning right at a T-junction and continuing up to emerge from the trees at the top.

Keep to the left of the buildings of Abberley Hall – now a school – to a T-junction, turn right along a broad track and where it bends right, keep ahead, at a public footpath sign 'Worcestershire Way', along a track that passes to the left of the Clock Tower [A]. As you descend to a road, there are impressive views to the left across the broad Teme valley to the line of the Clee Hills. Turn left along the road, take the right-hand road at a fork and after a quarter of a mile (0.4km), turn right onto a track, at a public footpath sign to Abberley Village. Continue along the left edge of a field, by an iron fence, and in the field corner keep ahead along a gently descending path to go through a kissing gate onto a lane.

Turn right, turn left at a public footpath sign and take a tarmac path across a field towards Abberley church. Go through a kissing gate on the far side to the left of the church, [B] keep ahead along a lane and at a public footpath sign, turn right along a drive. Walk in front of a house and on across grass to climb a stile and continue along the right edge of a field. Climb a stile in the fence on the right and head across a field corner to climb another one. Ahead is a fine view of Abberley Hill. Continue downhill across a field, climb a stile at the bottom, keep in the same direction across the next field and in the corner of it climb a stile onto a lane.

Turn right uphill to reach the square in Abberley village and the Norman church [C]. In the square turn first left and then almost immediately right onto an uphill track, at a public footpath sign to Wynniatts Way. At a footpath post, turn left over a stile and a few yards ahead – there is a Worcestershire Way post here – turn right and head uphill. Climb another stile, keep ahead to climb two more stiles in quick succession and continue uphill along the right edge of a field. Climb a stile in the field corner and continue steeply uphill through woodland, finally climbing steps to emerge onto a lane.

Turn right uphill and at a public footpath sign 'Worcestershire Way North', turn left over a stile. Continue winding uphill through the trees, following the regular Worcestershire Way signs, to reach the trig point on the summit of Abberley Hill. At a height of 930 feet (283m) – the highest point between the Malvern and Clee hills – it is inevitably a superb viewpoint, with Woodbury Hill prominent to the south. Now follows a splendid ridge walk along the wooded hilltop, descending steadily and still following the frequent Worcestershire Way signs. At one point, a gap in the trees on the right reveals a fine view of Abberley Clock Tower and the ruins of Witley Court. Keep along the ridge as far as a yellow-waymarked post where a path can be seen leading off to the right by wooden palings. (If you miss this turning point and reach a blue-waymarked post, simply retrace your steps to the last yellow-waymarked post). Turn right onto the path which descends steeply through woodland. Go through a gate, continue downhill along a sunken path, cross a track and keep ahead down a tree-lined path to a road. Turn left, take the first turning on the right and at a public foot-

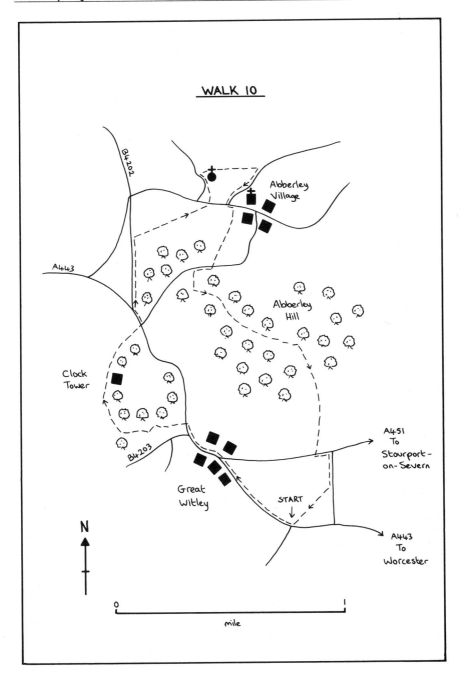

WALK 10

path sign, turn right through a hedge gap. Follow a path diagonally across a field, go through a kissing gate in the corner and turn right along the road to the start.

Features of Interest

A. The tall, ornate Clock Tower, known locally as 'Jones' Folly', is 161 feet high and a major landmark, visible for miles around. It was built in 1883 by John Joseph Jones of nearby Abberley Hall in memory of his father.

B. This imposing Victorian church, first built in 1850 and then rebuilt in 1876 after a fire, replaced the ruined old church in the village centre.

C. It is an unexpected pleasure to come across this little Norman church, built in the 12th century and extended two centuries later. After a long period of neglect, it fell into ruin but instead of being restored, the new church was built on a different site to the north of the village. The old church continued to decay but a programme of partial restoration began in 1963 and what basically remains today is the chancel – in which services are still held – plus the foundations and two doorways from the original Norman church.

Abberley village

11. Woodbury Hill and Witley Court

Start/Parking: Great Witley, Village Hall car park – grid reference 757657

Distance: The full walk is 6½ miles (10.5km), the shorter version which omits the detour to Witley Court and church is 4½ miles (7.2km)

Category: Fairly strenuous

Refreshments: Light refreshments at Witley Court

Terrain: Two climbs and descents, some of the paths are likely to be muddy and uneven, detour to Witley Court and church is along a flat track

OS Maps: Landranger 150, Explorer 204

Public transport: None

Explore & Discover

From Great Witley the route heads up over the wooded slopes of Woodbury Hill; part of the Abberley range, site of a prehistoric fort and a fine viewpoint. An easy descent back to the start is followed by an optional, but highly worthwhile detour to the imposing and atmospheric ruins of Witley Court and the adjoining flamboyant, 18th-century church.

Route Directions

Turn right out of the car park and take the first road on the left, signposted to Martley. At a public footpath sign, turn right along a track and pass to the right of a pool to reach a gate. Go through, almost immediately bear right to go through another one and walk across a field to a stile in the hedge in front. Climb two stiles in quick succession, continue across the next field to climb a stile on the far side, keep alongside a wire fence on the left and climb another stile onto a lane.

Turn right along the lane to a road, turn left uphill and just before a slight right bend, turn left, at a public footpath sign, to a stile. Climb it, keep ahead beside a pool on the right to climb another and continue along the left edge of a sloping field towards a farm, picking up a track. The track keeps to the right of the farm buildings and in front of the farmhouse – just before the track curves left and above a pool on the left – bear right to pass through a fence gap (in the absence of a stile at the time of writing). Head uphill across a field, making for a hedge corner on the far side, continue along the left edge of the next field, by a hedge on the left, and before reaching the field corner, walk beneath an avenue of trees to a stile.

Climb it, continue along the bottom inside edge of sloping woodland, climb another stile on the far side of the wood and head downhill across a field to climb a stile on the far side. Continue across the next field, climb a stile in the far corner and keep ahead along the top edge of a field towards another farm. Turn right through a gate by the farm buildings, head uphill along the left edge of a field and after going over the brow, descend to climb a stile into woodland. Bear right downhill and, at a Worcestershire Way post, turn sharp left and continue down through the trees, turning right near the bottom to a lane. Both on the descent and on reaching the lane, you enjoy grand views across the Teme valley to the Clee Hills.

Turn left and at a public footpath sign, turn left again through gates onto a tarmac drive. Where this drive bends sharply to the left, keep ahead into woodland and the path heads uphill and bends left to a stile. After climbing it, continue uphill through dark and gloomy conifers, climb a stile on the far side and keep ahead towards another stile. Do not climb this one but turn left to climb a stile and continue along a track. Now come impressive views to the right across the valley to the distant outline of the Malverns. Just before the track curves left to a farm, turn right over a stile and turn left across a field to climb another stile on the edge of the trees below Woodbury Hill.

Bear right along an attractive track which keeps along the bottom inside edge of the woodland and after going through a gate, turn left along an uphill path through the trees. The well-waymarked path continues uphill along the right edge of woodland, curving first right and then turning left to head over the thickly-wooded summit of Woodbury Hill, 904 feet (275m) high [A]. At the top bear left to continue along a broad track which later descends. The track keeps more or less in a straight line but you do need to keep a look out for the regular waymarks. Near the bottom the track narrows to a path and continues down to a lane. Turn left and, at a public footpath sign, turn right over a stile, here picking up the outward route, and retrace your steps to the start.

For the detour to Witley Court and church, keep ahead past the car

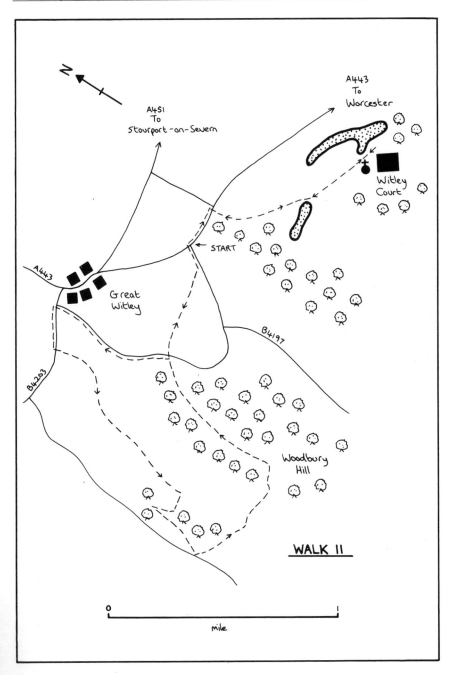

N

A451
To
Stourport-on-Severn

A443
To
Worcester

A443

Great
Witley

START

Witley
Court

B4197

B4203

Woodbury
Hill

WALK II

0   1

mile

Witley Court

park and turn right along the track signposted to Witley Church. You reach the church [B] after 1 mile (1.6km) and the ruined house is just beyond [C]. Return by the same route to the start.

Features of Interest

A. There is an Iron Age fort on Woodbury Hill but its site is obscured by the crown of trees and difficult to make out. During the Welsh rebellion led by Owain Glendwr in the early 15th century, Glendwr's army is alleged to have occupied the hill, facing the rival forces of Henry IV who were camped on the opposite Abberley Hill. (See Walk 10) Both armies apparently withdrew without conflict.

B. The church was built in 1735 by Lord Foley. After the rather plain exterior, the unusually rich and ornate interior comes as something of a surprise and with its white and gold colouring, painted ceiling and 18th-century stained glass windows, it resembles the Baroque churches of Austria and Bavaria. Miraculously it emerged virtually unscathed from the fire that engulfed the adjacent house.

C. An English Heritage leaflet proclaims Witley Court as 'the most spectacular ruined house in England' and what a splendid sight it must have been when complete and in its heyday, surrounded by elaborate landscaped gardens. After purchasing the estate, Lord Ward, the first Earl of Dudley, had the original 17th-century manor house transformed around 1860 into a vast Italian-style palace but it was badly damaged by a disastrous fire in 1937 and subsequently abandoned. Even in ruins the house still has an air of elegance and grandeur and the finest views are of the imposing south front from near the Poseidon Fountain. The grounds, with their ornamental gardens, great fountains, lake and woodlands, are currently being restored to something like their former glory and the work should be completed by the year 2001.

12. Hartlebury Common and Stourport-on-Severn

Start/Parking: Leapgate Country Park, Hartlebury Common, Wilden Top car park, off B4193 (Hartlebury-Stourport road) – grid reference 825714

Distance: The full walk is 7 miles (11.3km); the shorter version which omits the detour to Hartlebury village and castle is 6 miles (9.7km)

Category: Moderate

Refreshments: White Hart at Hartlebury, Orchard Café at Hartlebury Castle, Bird in Hand just after joining the canal towpath, pubs and cafés at Stourport-on-Severn, Old Rose and Crown on edge of Hartlebury Common near the end

Terrain: The woodland and heathland of the common at the beginning and end; in between field paths, tracks, lanes, disused railway track and canal towpath

OS Maps: Landranger 138, Explorer 219

Public Transport: Buses from Stourport-on-Severn and Hartlebury

Explore & Discover

There is plenty of variety on this walk. From the elevated and open expanses of Hartlebury Common, you descend to the edge of Hartlebury followed by an optional – and thoroughly recommended – detour into the village and on to the castle, the palace of the bishops of Worcester. The route continues, first along a disused railway line and then the towpath of the Staffordshire and Worcestershire Canal, into the canal town of Stourport-on-Severn. A short stretch of riverside walking brings you to the edge of the common and a short climb leads back to the start.

Route Directons

Start by the Countryside Information Board and head across to the trig point [A]. Walk past it and just before a yellow-waymarked post, the track narrows to a path and continues gently downhill along the right edge of a field. Cross a track, continue downhill and in the field corner – at the base of an embankment – turn right over a stile.

Walk across a field, passing under a pylon, climb a stile in the corner and continue below the wooded embankment, climbing a series of stiles, to reach Hillditch Pool. Eventually the path curves left around the end of the pool to emerge onto a narrow lane. Turn left, at a T-junction turn left again and take the first turning on the right to continue along another narrow lane to where a public footpath crosses it – there are signs on both sides of the lane.

Turn left over a stile here if doing the shorter walk which omits the detour into Hartlebury village and on to the castle.

For the full walk, continue along the lane to a T-junction in Hartlebury, [B] turn left and turn right along the drive to the castle [C].

Retrace your steps to where the detour began and turn right over a stile – here rejoining the shorter route. Walk across a field, bear left on the far side and at a hedge corner, bear right to continue across the next field. Descend steps to a lane and keep ahead to a T-junction. From here there is an impressive view of Hartlebury Castle across a pool. Turn left at the T-junction and where the road bears left, turn right onto Charlton Lane and almost immediately bear left along a straight, hedge-lined track. The track continues between fields and ascends gently to cross a bridge over the track of the disused Leapgate Old Railway [D].

Just after crossing the bridge, turn left down to the track and turn right along it. Follow it alternately through attractive wooded cuttings and across embankments – crossing high above the River Stour at one point – to where it ends at a bridge over the Staffordshire and Worcestershire Canal. Do not cross the bridge but turn right down steps to the towpath and turn sharp left to pass under the bridge. Continue beside the canal into Stourport as far as York Street Lock where the towpath emerges onto a road. Cross the road to the left of the canal bridge and walk down Mart Lane, passing to the left of the canal basins, to the River Severn [E].

Turn left along a tarmac riverside path – briefly joining the Severn Way – cross a footbridge at the confluence of the Severn and Stour and continue beside the river. At the far end of a meadow and in front of a white house, turn left to keep along the right edge of the meadow and the path joins a lane. Continue along it between houses and just after passing a 50 mph sign, turn right onto a path that heads across the edge of Hartlebury Common to a road. Cross over and take the path ahead through the trees, grassland and gorse of the common. The path later continues to the right of garden fences and bears right to reach a cross-roads of paths to the right of a public footpath sign.

The final part of the walk is potentially confusing as there are many paths – mostly unmarked – across the common and therefore you need to pay careful attention to the route directions. If you do inadvertently stray off the described route, simply aim for the highest point and you are bound to end up at the start.

At the crossroads, keep ahead across grass to another crossroads a few yards ahead and keep ahead again along a sandy path which climbs gently through gorse bushes to reach an open grassy area. Bear slightly left across it, continue uphill between heather, gorse and trees – later between embankments – and near the top, turn right to a T-junction immediately in front. Turn left to emerge onto the top of the common – passing under electricity cables – and on reaching a track, turn left along it and head across more open country to return to the start.

Stourport-on-Severn

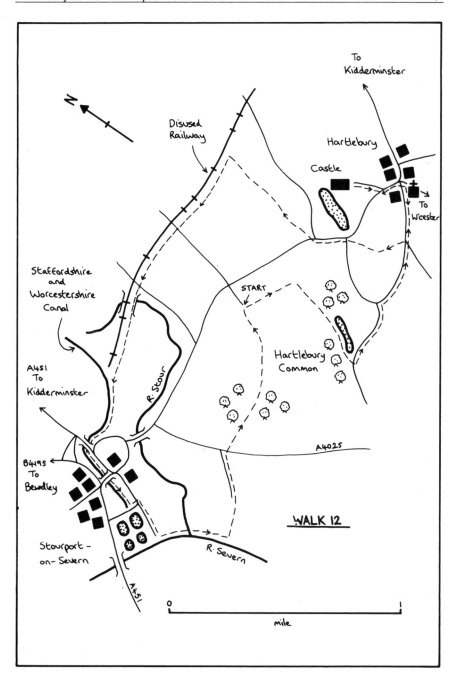

N

To Kidderminster

Disused Railway

Hartlebury

Castle

To Wcester

Staffordshire and Worcestershire Canal

START

A451 To Kidderminster

R. Stour

Hartlebury Common

A4025

B4195 To Bewdley

WALK 12

Stourport-on-Severn

R. Severn

A451

0   1

mile

Features of Interest

A. The main component of Leapgate Country Park is the 216 acres of Hartlebury Common but it also includes the 11 acres of pool and woodland at Hillditch Pool and Coppice, plus the track of the disused Leapgate Old Railway. Hartlebury Common is a rare surviving example of lowland heathland in the Midlands and comprises a mixture of heath, open grassland, scrub, bog and woodland. Although the trig point stands at the modest height of only 184 feet (56m), the views over the surrounding countryside are both impressive and extensive.

B. There are some attractive, if unassuming, brick cottages and a few half-timbered buildings in Hartlebury village. Apart from the imposing late 16th-century tower, the church was mostly rebuilt in 1836-37.

C. Since the Middle Ages, Hartlebury Castle has been the palace of the bishops of Worcester. The medieval castle was almost totally destroyed by fire in 1646 – during the Civil War – and was rebuilt in the late 17th and 18th centuries. Part of the castle now houses the Worcestershire County Museum and the impressive state rooms of the bishop's palace are open at times.

D. The Leapgate Old Railway linked the Severn Valley Railway near Bewdley with the Kidderminster-Worcester line near Hartlebury. It now provides about 2 miles (3.2km) of easy, flat and pleasant walking.

E. Stourport-on-Severn is a unique creation of the canal era; the only town in England to come into existence as the result of the building of a canal. In 1771 the Staffordshire and Worcestershire Canal, designed by Brindley, was opened to provide a link between the Trent and Mersey Canal and the River Severn and Stourport began to develop at the point where the canal emptied into the river. Growth was initially rapid but the town declined soon after the construction in 1815 of a new direct canal link between the industrial Midlands and the River Severn – the Worcester and Birmingham Canal – and the later development of the railways.

Some fine Georgian architecture survives from Stourport's canal heyday, especially the grand Tontine Hotel built in 1773, and a stroll around the complex of canal basins and lock systems between York Street and the river is an interesting and rewarding experience.

13. Avoncroft, Tardebigge and Stoke Prior

Start/Parking: Avoncroft Picnic Place, signposted from A38 2 miles (3.2km) south of Bromsgrove – grid reference 954685

Distance: 8 miles (12.9km)

Category: Moderate

Refreshments: Tearoom at Avoncroft Museum, Tylers Lock beside the canal, Queens Head at Stoke Pound Bridge, Navigation Inn at Stoke Prior, Ewe and Lamb near the end

Terrain: A mainly flat walk, initially along field paths and quiet lanes, with almost 3½ miles (5.6km) along a canal towpath

OS Maps: Landrangers 150 and 139, Explorer 204

Public Transport: Buses from Bromsgrove and Droitwich

Explore & Discover

Starting next to the Avoncroft Museum of Historic Buildings, the route takes you across fields and along quiet lanes to the Worcester and Birmingham Canal at Tardebigge. After a brief climb to the fine hilltop church, whose needle-like spire is in sight for much of the way, you continue along the canal towpath, passing the well-known Tardebigge Flight of Locks, to Stoke Wharf. At Stoke Prior, another interesting church can be visited and a final stretch along the edge of the Avoncroft complex leads back to the start.

Route Directions

The walk starts at the car park and picnic place adjoining the Avoncroft Museum of Historic Buildings [A]. Turn right out of the car park along a lane and in front of a railway bridge, turn left along a tarmac path, between a fence on the left and the railway line on the right. After half a mile (0.8km), the path bends left to emerge onto a lane. Turn right and right again to cross a bridge over the railway, climb a stile and walk along the left edge of a field.

About half-way along, turn left, at yellow waymarks, into the next field, keep along its left edge, climb a stile in the corner and continue, first along an enclosed path and then along a tarmac drive, to a lane. Bear right along it (Dusthouse Lane), keep ahead at a junction, in the Tardebigge direction, and continue along the lane for 1¼ miles (2km). Where it turns left, keep ahead, at a public footpath sign, across a field, descending into a slight hollow where you turn right to cross a plank footbridge over a ditch. Walk along an enclosed path, climb a stile, bear right across a field, cross another plank footbridge and head up an embankment to climb another stile. Bear left uphill across a field to a stile near a fence corner, climb it, continue uphill, climb a stile in the far corner of the field and cross a canal bridge. Do not climb the stile in front but turn sharp left and descend steps to the towpath of the Worcester and Birmingham Canal.

At this point the route continues to the left but a brief and eminently satisfying detour to the right enables you to visit and enjoy the fine views from Tardebigge church. Just after passing Top Lock House, turn right over a stile, head uphill and a stile in the field corner admits you to the churchyard [B].

Return to the canal towpath, turn left and keep along it for the next 3½ miles (5.6km). This pleasant and attractive stretch of canal walking takes you along the length of the famed Tardebigge flight of locks [C] and passes to the right of Tardebigge Reservoir. You leave the canal at bridge 44 (Stoke Wharf) and turn right over the bridge. Walk along the road and turn right along Fish House Lane by Stoke Prior church [D]. Follow the lane around a left bend and at a right bend, turn left along a track. Pass by cottages, continue along an enclosed path, cross a bridge over the River Salwarpe and follow this hedge-lined path – later a track – to rejoin the road opposite the Ewe and Lamb.

Continue along the road and at a public footpath sign, turn right through a kissing gate, bear slightly right and walk across a field, joining and keeping by a wire fence on the right. The path bends first right and then left and passes to the right of the windmill at Avoncroft to reach a kissing gate. Go through, head across a field, go through a gate in the left corner and continue along a track to another gate. After going through that, follow a track between farm buildings, go through one more gate and keep ahead to a lane. Turn left to return to Avoncroft.

Features of Interest

A. The diverse collection of buildings at Avoncroft have been brought from all over the Midlands and re-erected on this site to form a fascinating outdoor museum. The collection includes a superb 14th-cen-

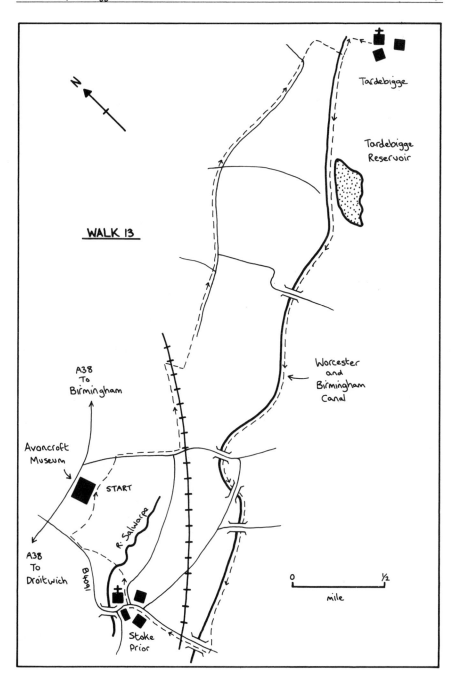

WALK 13

tury roof from the former Prior's guest hall at Worcester, ice house, dovecote, toll house, 15th-century Merchant's House, medieval cruck-framed barn, nailshop and chainshop, working windmill, Victorian corrugated iron chapel and even a 1946 Birmingham pre-fab. Avoncroft also houses the National Telephone Kiosk collection. Allow plenty of time, for there is lots to see.

B. This simple but elegant Georgian hilltop church was built in the 1770s following the collapse of its medieval predecessor. The slender spire, a landmark throughout much of the walk, is 135 feet high. From the churchyard the superb and extensive views include the tower and spire of Bromsgrove church and the line of the Malverns on the horizon.

C. The Worcester and Birmingham Canal was built between 1794 and 1815 to link the industrial Midlands with the River Severn. In its 30-mile length, it drops 453 feet (138m) by means of 58 locks. The Tardebigge Locks are the longest flight of locks in the country.

Top Lock, Tardebigge

D. The architecturally fascinating Stoke Prior church is one of Worcestershire's largely unknown gems. Apart from a more recent spire, most of it dates from around 1200, a period of transition between the Norman and early Gothic styles. The rounded Norman arches of the north arcade of the nave and south doorway contrast with the narrow pointed lancet windows of the Gothic style seen on the tower.

14. Lickey Hills

Start/Parking: Lickey Hills Country Park Visitor Centre, off B4096 a quarter of a mile (0.4km) east of Lickey church – grid reference 996754

Distance: 4½ miles (7.2km)

Category: Fairly strenuous

Refreshments: Café at Visitor Centre; cafés, restaurants and the Old Hare and Hounds at Rednal; café by Golf Club car park

Terrain: Woodland and open hillside, with three fairly steep climbs

OS Maps: Landranger 139, Explorer 219

Public Transport: Buses from Bromsgrove, Halesowen and Redditch pass Lickey church; the walk could also be started from Rednal which is served by buses from Birmingham

Explore & Discover

Traditionally the Lickey Hills were the most popular Sunday afternoon and Bank Holiday destination for the citizens of Birmingham, especially in the days when most people used public transport. The walk takes you over four of the hills that make up this relatively small though highly attractive, well-wooded and quite steep range that rises to 975 feet (298m). From the higher points the contrasting views take in a large slice of Birmingham and extend across rural Worcestershire to the distant Cotswold and Malvern hills.

Route Directions

Start in front of the Visitor Centre [A] and turn right up to the lower car park. Turn right again along a broad track and at a fork, take the right-hand track – passing beside a wooden barrier – into the trees. The track heads downhill through the delightful Cofton Woods, curving left to a T-junction at the bottom. Turn right parallel to a road on the left and at the next T-junction, turn left to emerge onto the road.

Turn right, almost immediately turn left along Cofton Church Lane and follow it to the church [B]. From here, walk back along the lane to the first public footpath sign and turn right over a stile to join the North

Worcestershire Path. Head gently uphill along the right edge of a field, at a North Worcestershire Path post turn left and continue across the field to climb a stile. Do not climb the stile immediately ahead but turn right onto an enclosed tarmac track which continues across a dam between two small reservoirs. Go through a gate, keep ahead to a road and continue along it to a T-junction.

Turn left uphill and over the brow of the hill, turn right onto a tarmac path which heads across the open expanse of Cofton Park, turning left to emerge onto a road at Rednal [C]. Cross over, take the uphill track opposite and follow it as it turns right to continue gently uphill through woodland over Rednal Hill to a T-junction. Turn left, take the first path on the right and almost immediately turn right again – at a waymarked post – onto a path which bears left and descends steeply through trees and bushes to a track. Cross over, keep ahead to emerge from the trees and bear right at a waymarked post to keep along the edge of a golf course. Continue straight ahead across the course, later bearing slightly left and aiming for the right-hand corner of woodland. Here you pick up a distinct path again which heads gently uphill along the right inside edge of the trees, becoming steeper and bearing left to a crossroads. Turn right up steps – here rejoining the North Worcestershire Path – and continue steeply up to emerge onto the open, grassy summit of Beacon Hill. After passing a trig point, keep ahead across the grass to the elaborate, battlemented viewing platform which, at 975 feet (298m), is the highest point on the Lickeys. Retrace your steps down to the crossroads where you joined the North Worcestershire Path, turn right and at a T-junction, turn left downhill. At the next North Worcestershire Path post a few yards ahead, turn right and at the next one, turn left down steps and continue across grass to pass to the left of a bowling green into the golf club car park. From here follow more waymarks through a rose garden to the road.

Cross over, go up the steps opposite, at a footpath sign to Lickey Hills Visitor Centre, and at an immediate fork, take the left-hand path to climb the 'Hundred Steps' up Bilberry Hill. The view from here, looking back towards Beacon Hill, is particularly memorable. Continue across the top of the hill and take the right-hand path at a fork which leads back to the upper car park. Turn right across it down to the lower car park and continue back to the Visitor Centre.

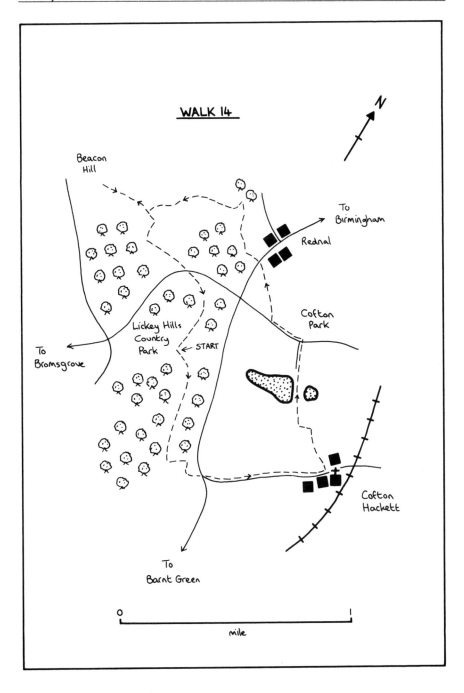

WALK 14

Beacon Hill

To Birmingham

Rednal

Cofton Park

Lickey Hills Country Park

← START

To Bromsgrove

Cofton Hackett

To Barnt Green

0   1
mile

Features of Interest

A. Although only designated a country park in 1971, the Lickey Hills
have been a popular recreation area since 1888 when Rednal Hill
was given to the city of Birmingham. Over the subsequent years,
gifts from the Cadbury family and purchases from the Earl of Plym-
outh extended the area to the present 524 acres, comprising mixed
woodlands, heathland and grassland. The main ridge of the Lickeys
– Cofton, Bilberry and Rednal hills – supports the largest tract of bilberry heathland in Worcestershire and the West Midlands. From
many points on the hills, the extensive views take in both the suburbs of Birmingham and rural Worcestershire.

B. Originally a chapel, the small church at Cofton Hackett was mostly
rebuilt in 1861 but retains some of its original medieval work. The
timber porch and bell turret both date from the 15th century

C. The path emerges onto the road by the site of the old Rednal tram ter-
minus. In the heyday of the Lickeys as a major attraction for
Brummies, this was the main arrival and departure point and on fine
Sunday or Bank Holiday evenings, there would be immense queues
of people waiting for the endless line of trams that used to turn round
here and take them back to Birmingham city centre.

15. Forge Mill and Arrow Valley Park

Start/Parking: Forge Mill Needle Museum and Bordesley Abbey Visitor Centre, off A441 (Birmingham-Redditch road) on the northern edge of Redditch — grid reference 045686

Distance: 4½ miles (7.2km)

Category: Easy

Refreshments: Café at new Arrow Valley Park Visitor Centre (when fully open in spring 2000)

Terrain: Flat walking across meadows, parkland and around a lake, much of the route on tarmac paths

OS Maps: Landranger 150, Explorer 220

Public transport: Buses from Birmingham, Redditch and Evesham

Explore & Discover

There is considerable historic interest on this walk, much of which is beside water; either the River Arrow, Arrow Valley Lake or one of the numerous brooks, channels and mill ponds. It starts at a museum to Redditch's major industry and by the sparse remains of a medieval abbey, and takes you across a narrow but attractive wedge of open country that has survived amidst suburban expansion to the Arrow Valley Park. After a circuit of the lake, you retrace your steps to the start.

Route Directions

Turn left in front of the gates to the museum, [A] cross a footbridge, go through a gate and turn right along the edge of part of Bordesley Abbey Meadows. The few visible remains of the abbey are over to the left. In the corner of the meadow, follow the path to the right across a footbridge, turn left and continue along the left edge of more meadowland, now with the River Arrow on the left. About 50 yards (46m) before the corner, turn left to cross a footbridge over the river, turn right and shortly turn right over another footbridge. Continue along a tree-lined path with water on both sides - there are boardwalks in places - and later the channel on the left broadens out into a mill pond. At a T-junction, turn right to join a tarmac track - both a footpath and cycle way - which keeps by the river on the right all the while. Bear right at the next junction to pass under a road bridge, turn left by a small triangular green and bear right again to pass under another road bridge.

Cross a road, pass between a barrier and keep ahead as far as the second footbridge on the right. Just before reaching it, turn sharp left onto another tarmac track and follow it around the Arrow Valley Lake. After passing the new Visitor Centre [B] – not yet completed at the time of writing – turn right at a crossroads at the north-east corner of the lake, turn right again at a T-junction and continue along the lake's east side. On reaching the far, tapering south end, turn right and right again and walk back along the west side to complete the circuit.

At the north-west corner you rejoin the outward route and retrace your steps to the start.

Features of Interest

A. There are two buildings to visit on the museum site. One is Forge Mill Needle Museum which tells the story of the Redditch needle industry, describing how the needles were made, the machinery that was used, the social conditions of the workers and why the industry became concentrated in the Redditch area. The latter is not easy to explain but the proximity of the resources of the Black Country was undoubtedly a significant factor.

The other building is a modern Visitor Centre which contains objects found in the excavation of nearby Bordesley Abbey and displays on the abbey's history. Most of the abbey remains unexcavated but a few of the foundations are visible in an enclosure across the meadow to the north of the museum. It was a Cistercian monastery, founded in 1138.

B. The 900-acre Arrow Valley Park is an extremely valuable open space amidst the ring roads and modern suburban expansion of Redditch. The lake is particularly popular for fishing and boating. At the time of writing, a new Visitor Centre is being built at the north-east corner of the lake and is scheduled to be fully open in the spring of 2000. It will have refreshment facilities.

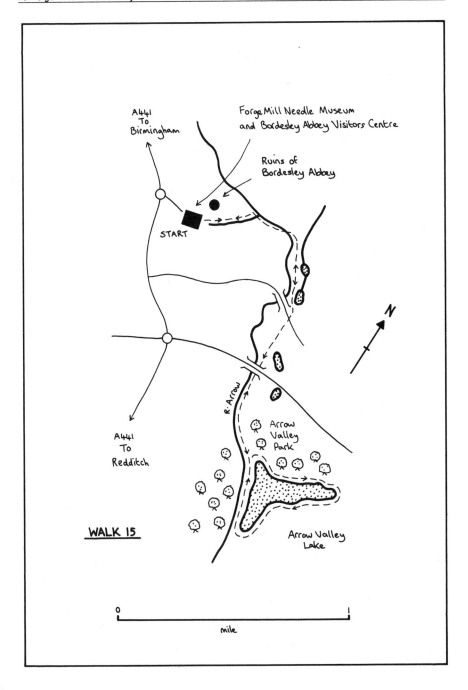

A441
To
Birmingham

Forge Mill Needle Museum
and Bordesley Abbey Visitors Centre

Ruins of
Bordesley Abbey

START

N

A441
To
Redditch

R. Arrow

Arrow
Valley
Park

WALK 15

Arrow Valley
Lake

0   1
mile

16. Feckenham and Inkberrow

Start/Parking: Feckenham – grid reference 008615

Distance: 7½ miles (12.1km)

Category: Moderate

Refreshments: Rose and Crown and Lygon Arms at Feckenham, Bulls Head and Old Bull at Inkberrow

Terrain: Tracks, field paths and lanes with some gentle climbing, likely to be muddy stretches in places

OS Maps: Landranger 150, Explorer 220 and 205

Public transport: Buses from Worcester and Droitwich Spa

Explore & Discover

This walk is in the heart of the old Forest of Feckenham, one of the many medieval royal hunting grounds in the Midlands that have now mostly vanished, apart from a few isolated woods. The route links two highly attractive villages, both of which have appealing inns, village greens, picturesque cottages and fine medieval churches.

Route Directions

Turn left out of the car park along High Street and take the first turning on the left to walk through The Square, an attractive green bordered by a mixture of brick, whitewashed and timber-framed cottages. Feckenham church is to the right [A].

At the far end, continue along Mill Lane which becomes a straight, tree-lined track. Take the right track at a fork, passing to the right of a former mill, and go through a gate to the left of the mill pond. Walk along an enclosed path, cross a footbridge over Bow Brook and continue uphill. At a public bridleway sign, turn left along the path signposted 'Salt Way and Morton Underhill' which keeps above the brook to a gate [B]. Go through and keep ahead – now beside the brook – to emerge onto a road to the right of a bridge. Take the tarmac track ahead and where it bends right, keep ahead through a gate. Walk along the right edge of a

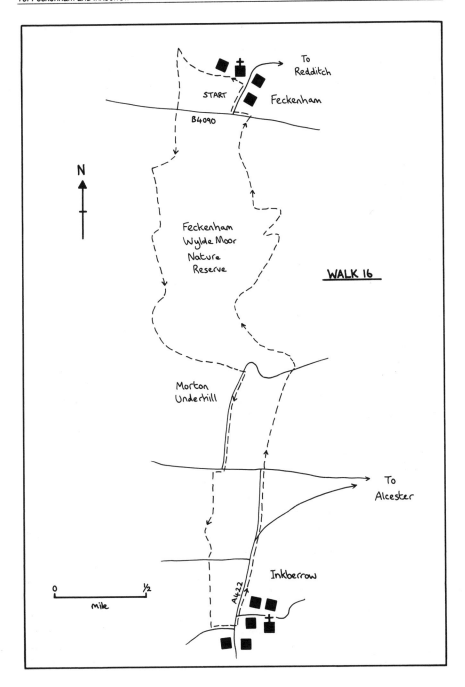

WALK 16

field, follow it to the right, go through a gate and continue along the right field edge. In the corner, turn left along a partially-enclosed path, go through a gate and the path turns first right – alongside a brook – and then left to cross a footbridge over the brook. Walk along the left edge of fields and at a waymarked post just before reaching the corner of the last field, bear left through a gate and continue along a broad, hedge-lined track to a lane in the hamlet of Morton Underhill. Turn right, follow this narrow lane steadily uphill to a road and turn right. At a public footpath sign, turn left up steps, climb a stile and walk along the left edge of a field to go through a gate. To the right is a fine view of the Malverns. Continue along the left field edge – later along a track – to a farm, go through a gate and on through the farmyard and another gate onto a lane. Cross over, continue along the left edge of a field – alongside houses – and just past the end of the hedgeline, turn right over a stile. Turn left along a broad track to climb another one and keep along the track to a road. Turn left to a T-junction and turn left again into Inkberrow. The first turnng on the right leads to a triangular green, picturesque Old Bull pub and medieval church [C]. Keep ahead through the village, bear left along Sands Road (signposted Village Hall) and at a T-junction, keep ahead through a gate and walk along an enclosed track. Where the track ends, go through a gate and keep ahead by a fence on the right which encloses a small reservoir. At the end of the fence, continue across the field, go through a gap in the hedge and line of trees on the far side and bear right across the next field. In the far corner, go through a gate and walk across the next field, keeping parallel to its left edge and making for another gate on the far side. After going through it, continue along a track, turn left over a stile at a public footpath sign and walk across a narrow field to climb another one. A few yards ahead, bear slightly left and head steeply downhill, passing through a hedge gap and keeping parallel to the left field edge, to climb a stile at the bottom. Turn right along a track, almost immediately turn left through a gate, walk along the left edge of a field and go through a gate at the far tapering end. Walk along the right edge of the next two fields and just before the corner of the second one, turn right through a gate and keep along the left edge of two more fields. In the corner of the second field, go through a gate and head straight across the next field, following the overhead cables to a gate on the far side. Go through, head across the field corner to go through the first gate on the left, cross a brook and bear left along a track. Go through a gate, walk in front of a barn and at the corner of the barn, turn right along a track.

After going through a gate, follow the track round a left bend to a T-junction and turn right. To the left is the Feckenham Wylde Moor Nature Reserve [D]. Head gently uphill to a road, turn left and turn right along High Street to return to the start.

The Old Bull, Inkberrow

Features of Interest

A. Feckenham lies at the heart of the former royal forest that was named after it. In the Middle Ages, the forest occupied the area roughly between Redditch, Worcester and Bromsgrove, with a northern extension towards Kidderminster. Over the centuries its trees were continuously felled to serve the salt industries of Droitwich and the iron industries of the Black Country and nowadays nothing of it survives, apart from a few isolated areas of woodland, such as Chaddesley Woods near Kidderminster. (see Walk 7).

The village is a pleasant mixture of old half-timbered cottages and dignified 18th-century brick houses, presided over by a much restored medieval church. The chancel was rebuilt in 1853.

B. The name of this track indicates the importance of salt in the medieval economy and it is one of many that ran across the Midlands from Droitwich, one of the principal centres of salt production.

C. Like Feckenham, Inkberrow is also an attractive mixture of half-timbered cottages and Georgian houses, with the added bonus of a picturesque pub, the Old Bull, which occupies one side of the triangular green. Nearby is the restored, mainly 15th-century church.

D. The nature reserve is what is left of the former Feckenham Bog, an area of pools, marsh and grassland. After being enclosed in 1832, an attempt was made to drain it for agricultural purposes but this was only partially successful. Now it is maintained by the Worcestershire Wildlife Trust as a valuable wetland site, rich in both flora and wildlife. There is public access but you are requested to keep to the marked footpaths.

17. Piper's Hill Common and Hanbury

Start/Parking: Car park just off the B4091 (Bromsgrove-Hanbury road), at corner of Holmes Lane on south side of Piper's Hill Common – grid reference 959648

Distance: 6 miles (9.7km)

Category: Moderate

Refreshments: Vernon Arms at Hanbury

Terrain: Well-waymarked route mainly along field paths and enclosed tracks, likely to be some muddy stretches

OS Maps: Landranger 150, Explorer 204

Public transport: Limited bus service from Droitwich Spa and Bromsgrove

Explore & Discover

This is a walk which combines fine scenery and outstanding views with considerable historic and architectural interest. From the wooded hilltop of Piper's Hill Common, you descend, via tracks and field paths, into the village of Hanbury. The route then continues up to the ridge, on which stands Hanbury Hall and – about half a mile (0.75km) further on – the isolated Hanbury church, in sight for much of the way and a superb viewpoint. From here a short stroll leads back to the start.

Route Directions

Emerging from the car park, [A] turn left along a track that keeps along the right edge of the wood, passing a thatched, black and white cottage, and at a crossroads of tracks, turn right through a gate beside a cattle-grid. Ahead is a fine view over the gentle countryside of east Worcestershire. Head downhill across grass – there is a concrete track to the left – and at the bottom, cross the track and keep ahead to go through a waymarked gate. Continue along the right edge of a field, go through two gates in quick succession and then keep along the left edge of an orchard to a stile. Climb it and walk along a hedge-lined track to a lane.

Keep ahead and where the lane bends left, turn sharp right through a gate and continue along an attractive, tree-lined bridleway. This may be muddy at times. The bridleway eventually emerges onto a lane. Bear left along it and where the lane bears left, keep ahead along a tarmac farm drive. After passing a farmhouse, turn right through a gate, walk along the right edge of a field, climb a stile and continue along the left edge of the next field to climb a stile in the corner. Head through a belt of trees into the next field, keep along its left edge, turn left over a stile in the field corner, climb another stile a few yards ahead and continue along the right edge of a field. Follow the winding field edge as far as a corner where you climb a stile. Go through a gate and keep ahead to emerge onto a road in Hanbury village, beside a petrol station and opposite the Vernon Arms. Turn right to a road junction, bear left, in the Droitwich direction, and at a public footpath sign, turn left along an enclosed path to a footbridge. After crossing it, keep ahead along the left edge of a field and in the corner turn right to continue along the left edge of three fields, climbing two stiles, to reach a footbridge. Cross it, keep ahead to climb a stile and continue across the next two fields, climbing a stile and making for a stile in the fence on the right-hand side of the second field. Climb it onto the road, cross over, go through a gate opposite and immediately climb another stile.

Head diagonally across a field, climb a stile in the far corner and descend steps to a lane. Turn right and at a public footpath sign, turn left up steps, climb a stile and walk across a field corner to a wire fence. Keep beside it, passing to the left of a farmhouse, and at the fence corner, keep straight ahead gently downhill across the field to a stile. Climb it – and another one immediately ahead – and walk across the next field, veering slightly left away from its right edge and aiming for a gap between two black and white cottages in front.

Go through a gate onto a lane, turn left to pass in front of one of the cottages and turn right through a gate onto a path which leads to a plank footbridge over a boggy area. After crossing it, continue across the field, keeping in line with the overhead power lines, climb a stile on the far side and bear slightly right across the next field to another stile. Climb it, turn right alongside a wire fence, climb a stile and keep ahead to go through a gate onto a road. Cross over, take the path opposite which heads up through a belt of trees and climb a stile to enter Hanbury Park. Turn half-left across a field to a stile, climb it and keep ahead for about 100 yards (91m) to the drive and entrance to Hanbury Hall [B].

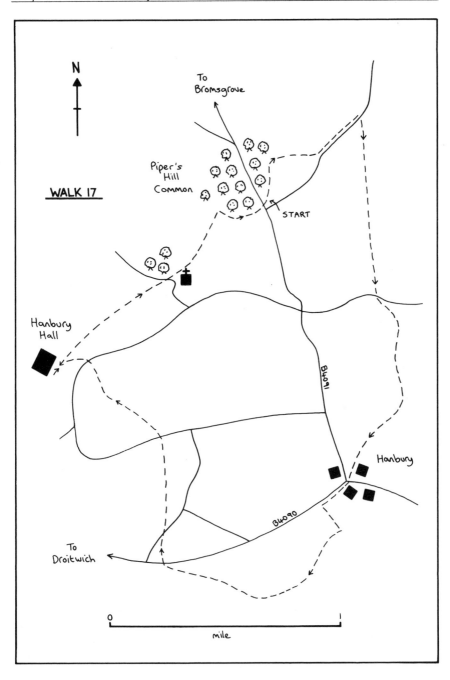

N

To
Bromsgrove

Piper's
Hill
Common

WALK 17

START

B4091

Hanbury
Hall

Hanbury

B4090

To
Droitwich

0   1
                mile

Retrace your steps to climb the previous stile again and continue in a straight line across the park – in the direction of Hanbury church – to a stile. Climb it, keep ahead beside a wire fence, follow the fence to the left and then turn right along a tree-lined avenue. Climb a stile, continue along the avenue, climb another stile and keep ahead gently uphill across a field towards the church. Go through a kissing gate, turn right along a lane and at a T-junction immediately in front, turn left up to Hanbury church [C]. Enter the churchyard, pass to the left of the church, go through a gate and take the path ahead which descends to a kissing gate. Go through, keep ahead to go through another one – here re-entering the woods of Piper's Hill Common – and walk along a track which bends right to keep along the bottom edge of the woodland. Look out for a yellow waymark at a gap in the trees on the left and take a path which heads quite steeply up to the hilltop. Continue through the trees, bearing right to keep by the right edge of the wooded crest, and the path emerges onto the road opposite the starting point.

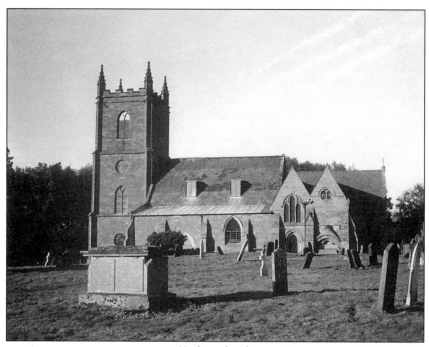

Hanbury church

Features of Interest

A. The woodland that crowns Piper's Hill Common contains some of the oldest and largest trees in the county, mostly beeches and sweet chestnuts with a few ancient oaks. It was mostly planted by the Vernon family of nearby Hanbury Hall and is now a wildlife reserve managed by Worcestershire Wildlife Trust. At a height of around 380 feet (116m), the common provides magnificent views over the surrounding countryside.

B. Hanbury Hall, a restrained and dignified brick-built house, was the home of the Vernon family. It dates from the beginning of the 18th century and was designed in the Wren style. The interior is particularly noted for the staircase and superb painted ceilings, and for the fine collection of porcelain and paintings. An unusual feature is the detached Long Gallery. There is also an impressive Orangery and 18th-century formal gardens.

C. Hanbury church occupies an isolated hilltop position about 1½ miles (2.4km) from the village. The hill commands extensive views over the surrounding countryside and was previously the site of an Anglo-Saxon monastery and possibly a prehistoric hillfort. The church was much altered in the 18th century, when the west tower was redesigned in a 'Georgian Gothic' style, and again in the 19th century when the chancel was rebuilt, but the interior of the nave is still basically medieval. There are monuments to the Vernons of the nearby hall.

18. Ombersley and Holt Fleet

Start: Ombersley, by the church – grid reference 845636

Distance: 6 miles (9.7km)

Category: Easy

Parking: Roadside parking at Ombersley

Refreshments: Crown and Sandys Arms and Kings Arms at Ombersley, Holt Fleet and Wharf Inn, plus Riverside Snack Bar (restricted opening) at Holt Fleet

Terrain: Lanes and field paths at the start and finish, otherwise most of the route is along riverside paths

OS Maps: Landranger 150, Explorer 204

Public transport: Buses from Worcester and Kidderminster

Ombersley

Explore & Discover

The black and white village of Ombersley makes a fine starting point for a walk that initially takes you across fields and along quiet lanes before descending into the Severn valley. An attractive path along the edge of riverside meadows leads to the bridge at Holt Fleet and you continue for a while beside the Severn before heading through woodland and across Ombersley Park to return to the start.

Route Directions

With the church on your left, walk up to the crossroads in the centre of Ombersley [A] and turn left. At a public bridleway sign, turn right along a track to a road, bear left along it and where it ends, keep ahead along a straight, hedge-lined, tarmac path. This path later widens into a track and continues to the corner of a lane. Turn left through the black and white hamlet of Uphampton, following the lane as it bends right to a T-junction.

Turn left and after a quarter of a mile (0.5km), bear right, at a public footpath sign, initially along a hedge-lined track and later along the left edge of fields, by a hedge on the left, descending gently and with grand views over the Severn valley ahead. In the field corner keep ahead to a lane, turn right and at a public footpath sign, turn left and head diagonally across a field, descending steps on the far side to a narrow lane. Turn left and where the lane bends left, keep ahead along a track. After passing to the left of farm buildings, the track becomes a tarmac one which descends towards the river. Near the bottom, look out for where you turn left over a stile, continue down to the bank of the River Severn and turn left.

You now follow the river to the bridge at Holt Fleet. This pleasantly tree-lined route – part of the Severn Way – keeps along the edge of riverside meadows, negotiates a succession of stiles and kissing gates and, after passing Holt Lock, continues along a tarmac drive. Before reaching the bridge, keep ahead along a path parallel to the drive, pass under the bridge and continue beside the river. The rest of the route back to Ombersley follows the Wychavon Way. There is another succession of stiles and the route passes in front of the Wharf Inn. On the other bank of the Severn, Holt Castle can be seen, with the top of the tower of Holt church peeping above the trees [B]. About 200 yards (183m) after climbing two stiles in quick succession, look out for a Wychavon Way sign where you turn left across the meadow to a stile on the edge of woodland. Climb it, head uphill through the wood and between embankments and on emerging from the trees, continue along a winding track. The track turns left across the end of a pool and at a Wychavon Way sign, turn right onto a wooded path that keeps initially along the left edge of the pool and continues along the right edge of a field. This part of the route is across Ombersley Park: to the right is woodland and across the field on the left are views of Ombersley Court and church. Climb a stile in the field corner, keep ahead across the next field, go through a gate and then a kissing gate and keep ahead to a road. Turn left through Ombersley to the start.

Features of Interest

A. Ombersley's main street is lined with attractive brick and timber-framed cottages, houses and inns. The church, built in the 1820s, has an imposing tower and spire and in the churchyard part of the chancel of its medieval predecessor survives as the mausoleum of the Sandys family of the adjacent Ombersley Court. The house, seen near the end of the walk, dates from the early 18th century and was refaced about a century later.

B. Holt Castle has been considerably extended and modernised over the centuries but retains an impressive medieval tower. As at Ombersley, house and church stand in close proximity in the traditional English manner. The church – well worth a visit – has been described as one of the finest Norman village churches in Worcestershire. Some of the 12th-century arches are particularly ornate.

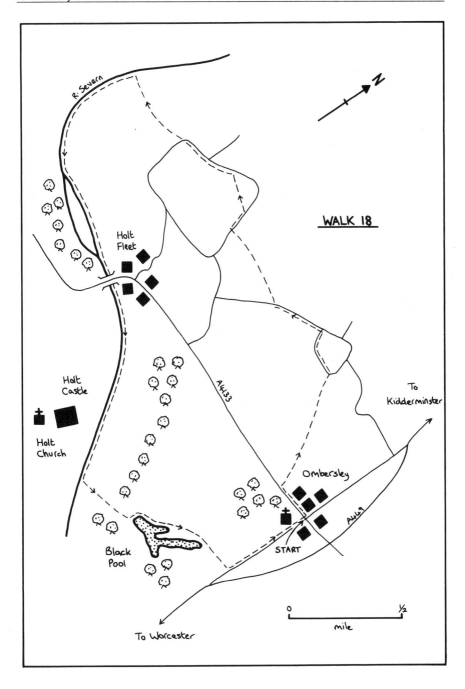

19. Worcester

Start: Guildhall – grid reference 851547

Distance: 2 miles (3.2km)

Category: Easy

Parking: Worcester

Refreshments: Plenty of places to eat and drink in Worcester

Terrain: Easy town walking

Maps: Pick up a street map from the Tourist Information Centre in the Guild-hall

Public Transport: Worcester is served by buses and trains from all the surrounding towns.

Explore & Discover

Situated at one of the principal crossing points on the River Severn, Worcester is one of the oldest cathedral cities in England and has been a major ecclesiastical and administrative centre since Anglo-Saxon times. In the Middle Ages its prosperity was based principally on cloth making but since the 18th century it has been particularly associated with the manufacture of high quality porcelain. The city played a leading role in the Civil War between King and Parliament and was the venue of what was effectively the last battle of that war in 1651. Although the medieval castle and city walls have long vanished and there has been considerable modern development in the centre, much of Worcester's history and many fine old buildings survive, principally, of course, the magnificent cathedral but also medieval and Tudor timber-framed houses, an early 18th-century Guildhall and Georgian streets and churches. Starting in front of the Guildhall, the walk takes you along some of the most attractive and historic streets – mostly now happily pedestrianised – to a Civil War Museum, on past the Royal Worcester Porcelain Works, through the cathedral precincts and along a stretch of the River Severn.

Worcester

Route Directions

With your back to the Guildhall, [A] turn left along the pedestrianised High Street and turn right into Church Street, passing St Swithun's, the first of a series of Georgian churches seen on the route. Cross The Shambles and continue along Mealcheapen Street into the Cornmarket. To the left is the brick-built, Old St Martin's church, constructed 1768-72, and on the corner of New Street is the half-timbered King Charles' House, in which Charles II allegedly hid from his enemies after his defeat at the Battle of Worcester in 1651. Turn right into New Street, a very attractive street with a number of black and white, half-timbered buildings, and keep ahead along the equally attractive Friar Street, passing Greyfriars on the left and, a little further on, the Museum of Local Life on the right [B]. At the bottom, turn left into College Street and continue along Sidbury, crossing the bridge over the Worcester and Birmingham Canal [C] to the Commandery Museum [D]. Recross the canal, turn left towards the Royal Worcester Porcelain Works and follow the road round to the right to a T-junction. To the left is the entrance to Royal Worcester [E]. At the T-junction, turn right and pass through the 14th-century Edgar Tower into College Green and the cathedral precincts. In order to gain access to the cathedral, [F] turn right to enter the cloisters. Return to the pleasant and tranquil surroundings of College Green, continue to the end and turn first left and then right down to the river. Descend steps, pass under the Water Gate and turn right along a tree-lined riverside path. Soon after passing in front of the cathedral, the isolated tower and spire of St Andrew's church can be seen over to the right [G]. Continue beside the Severn up to the elegant bridge – one of the best views of Worcester Cathedral is from this bridge – and turn right along Georgian Bridge Street [H]. Pass to the left of All Saints church, mostly built 1739-42, continue into the pedestrianised shopping area again and turn left into Angel Place. At a crossroads, turn right, passing the 19th-century Corn Exchange, and turn right again by the Georgian St Nicholas' church – now a café bar – along The Cross. Continue along High Street to return to the Guildhall.

Features of Interest

A. With its superb Queen Anne facade, the Guildhall is one of Worcester's most notable buildings. It was designed by Thomas White and built 1721-23. In the elegant surroundings of the Assembly Room you can enjoy a drink and a light meal.

B. These are two particularly outstanding timber-framed buildings. Greyfriars, built in 1480 and added to in the 17th and 18th centuries, is now maintained by the National Trust. It has fine panelled rooms and an attractive garden reached through an archway. The Museum of Local Life, housed in a 16th-century house, depicts the history of the city and people of Worcester.

C. Construction of the Worcester and Birmingham Canal began in 1794 and was completed in 1815. It linked the industrial Midlands with the Bristol Channel via Worcester and the River Severn.

D. This 15th-century timber-framed building was originally the Hospital of St Wulfstan. After the Reformation it became a house and during the Battle of Worcester in 1651, it served as the Royalist headquarters. Now the Commandery appropriately houses a museum to the English Civil War. Although the Civil War is usually regarded as ending with the execution of Charles I in 1649, the Battle of Worcester was effectively the final battle in that conflict. Charles II's defeat by Parliamentary forces ended his chances – for the time

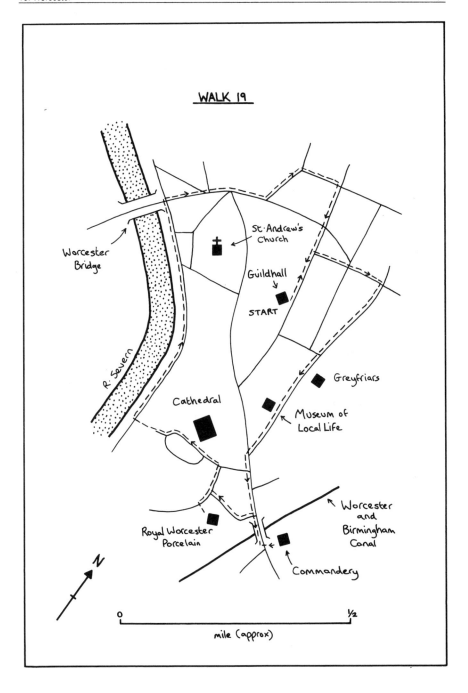

WALK 19

Worcester Bridge

St. Andrew's Church

Guildhall

START

R. Severn

Greyfriars

Cathedral

Museum of Local Life

Worcester and Birmingham Canal

Royal Worcester Porcelain

Commandery

N

0   ½

mile (approx)

being – of regaining the throne, forced him into exile and ensured that for the next nine years England would be a republic.

E. Royal Worcester claims to be the oldest continuous producer of porcelain. The factory was set up in 1751 and is particularly noted for its high quality Bone China. There is plenty to see and do here as there is a visitor centre, tours of the factory, museum, shops and a restaurant.

F. The diocese of Worcester was founded in the late 7th century but the present building was started in 1084 by Wulfstan, the only Saxon bishop to retain his seat after the Norman Conquest. A series of calamities – two fires and the collapse of a tower – destroyed most of Wulfstan's cathedral, apart from the superb Norman crypt, one of the finest in the country, and the chapter house. Reconstruction began around 1170 and was finally completed in 1374 with the building of the central tower. The tower and west front are the most striking features of the exterior, the former rising majestically above the Severn and looking particularly impressive when viewed either from the bridge or from the other side of the river. The east end dates mainly from the 13th century and the nave was mostly rebuilt in the 14th century. Two outstanding monuments in the cathedral are the tomb of King John before the high altar and Prince Arthur's Chantry. Arthur was the eldest son of Henry VII and first husband of Catherine of Aragon; but for his early death his younger brother, Henry VIII, might never have come to the throne or become Catherine's second husband.

G. The 15th-century tower and spire (the latter rebuilt in 1751) – rising to 245 feet – is all that remains of St.Andrew's church. The site is now occupied by an attractive garden flanked by the modern (1960s) buildings of Worcester College of Technology.

H. Both Worcester Bridge and Bridge Street – the latter conceived as an impressive approach to the former – were the work of John Gwynne and were built in the late 18th century.

20. Heart of Elgar Country

Start/Parking: Lower Broadheath, Memorial Hall car park – grid reference 811573

Distance: 5½ miles (8.9km)

Category: Easy

Refreshments: Plough near Elgar Birthplace Museum, Bell Inn at Lower Broadheath

Terrain: Field paths, tracks and lanes across mainly flat country

OS Maps: Landranger 150, Explorer 204

Public Transport: Buses from Worcester

Elgar's birthplace.

Explore & Discover

Virtually the whole of the area around Worcester and the Malverns can be described as 'Elgar Country' but this walk explores the lanes, tracks and paths in the immediate vicinity of Elgar's birthplace at Lower Broadheath. The birthplace, now a museum, can be visited but check opening times. From many points on the route, there are expansive views across the flat landscape to the encircling hills, especially the composer's beloved Malverns.

Route Directions

The car park is beside the church at Lower Broadheath [A]. Turn left out of the car park to the main road, turn right and almost immediately turn left along Frenchlands Lane. With views of the Malverns to the left and the Abberley Hills to the right, keep along this narrow lane for almost 1 mile (1.6km). It later becomes a rough track which continues to a farm. Pass between the farm buildings, turn left at the side of a brick building and turn right along an enclosed path – between fences – to a stile. Climb it and turn left along the left edge of the next three fields, climbing two stiles and finally climbing a third one onto a road. Turn left and on the brow of a small hill, turn right along the drive to Maple's Cross Farm. Walk through the farmyard, turn right around the end of stables and barns and then turn left along a track which enters a field. Keep along its left edge and in the corner, turn left over a stile and continue along a left field edge to another stile. Bear slightly left across a field, cross a ditch, go through a gate on the far side and veer slightly right across the next field, making for a hedge corner and beyond that a gap in a hedge. Go through, keep along the left field edge, follow it to the right and go through a gate onto a road.

Turn left, follow the road around a left bend and at a crossroads, turn right along Crown Lane East, in the Crown East, Worcester and Elgar Birthplace Museum direction. To the left are the wide, flat expanses of Broadheath Common. Walk past the Plough to the Elgar Birthplace Museum and at a public bridleway sign, turn left along a track beside the museum [B]. The track descends, then rises slightly and just before reaching a farm, turn left – there is a yellow waymark here – through a gap and follow a path across a field, heading gently downhill. Climb a stile on the far side, turn left beside a pool, turn right over a footbridge and keep ahead to climb a stile in a fence. Keep along the right field

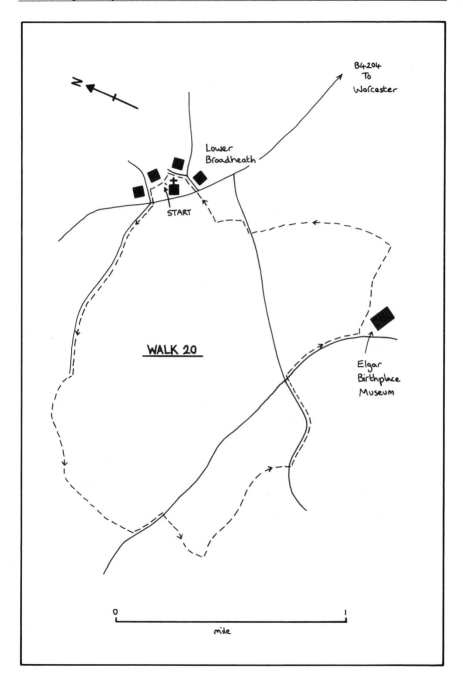

N

B4204
To
Worcester

Lower
Broadheath

START

WALK 20

Elgar
Birthplace
Museum

0

mile

edge, by a wire fence on the right, and at the fence corner, continue gently uphill to a stile. Climb it, bear slightly left across the next field to emerge onto a road by the side of a house and turn right. Take the first turning on the left (Partridge Lane) – which shortly becomes a track – and follow it, by a line of houses on the left, to where it ends. Turn right over a stile here and walk along a left field edge, curving slightly left to climb a stile onto a road.

The Plough is about 300 yards (274m) to the right. Keep ahead along Hallow Lane, turn left into Grange Road and where the road curves right, bear left along an enclosed tarmac track. Go through a kissing gate, follow a tarmac path along the left edge of a playing field and go through another kissing gate into the car park.

Features of Interest

A. The large and imposing church at Lower Broadheath was built in 1903-4.

B. Sir Edward Elgar, England's foremost composer, was born in 1857 in this modest cottage which faces his beloved Malvern Hills. It is now an Elgar museum and houses a unique collection of manuscripts, photographs, musical scores and concert programmes associated with his life and work. There is also personal memorabilia, including the desk at which he composed many of his greatest works. The museum is open throughout the year, except on Wednesdays and from the middle of January to the middle of February, but opening times vary.

21. Old Hills and Powick

Start/Parking: Old Hills car park, off B4424 (Powick-Upton upon Severn road) – grid reference 829487

Distance: 5½ miles (8.9km)

Category: Easy

Refreshments: Red Lion at Powick, Blue Bell and Old Bush at Callow End

Terrain: Field paths and tracks across gently sloping country

OS Maps: Landranger 150, Explorers 190 and 204

Public transport: Buses from Worcester and Great Malvern

Explore & Discover

The gentle slopes of the Old Hills are modest outliers of the Malverns and provide both superb and far reaching views. From the hills the route proceeds to the village of Powick, whose medieval church overlooks the confluence of the Severn and Teme, and continues by hopfields, past the 19th-century Stanbrook Abbey and through Callow End to return to the start.

The Malverns from Old Hills

Route Directions

Facing the Old Hills notice board, take the track to the right of it and head gently up to the triangulation pillar at the top, 230 feet (70m) high [A]. After appreciating the wide views, bear slightly right to keep along the left edge of the open grassland, by trees on the left, and head down-hill between gorse bushes, bearing slightly left and making for a gate where you join a track.

Immediately after going through the gate, turn right along a wide, hedge-lined track – likely to be muddy – to a lane. Turn right and at the second public footpath sign on the left, turn sharp left up steps to climb a stile and walk across a field towards a farm. Climb a stile on the far side, descend steps and turn right along an enclosed track. Just after passing through the farmyard, turn right through a gate, head downhill to go through another one and continue gently downhill, going through two more gates in quick succession and keeping ahead towards a farm. Go through a kissing gate, continue along a tarmac track, passing be-tween the farm buildings, and follow it to a road. Turn right into Powick, take the right-hand road at a fork and turn right at a T-junction in front of the Red Lion. At a public footpath sign, turn left along the tree-lined drive to Powick church, [B] go through a gate into the church-yard and turn right in front of the church to emerge from the church-yard via a kissing gate. Continue across a field, climb a stile and keep ahead along the left edge of a hopfield. At the corner of the field, climb a stile, continue along an enclosed path, climb two more stiles in quick succession and keep ahead to cross a footbridge over a brook. Walk across the next field, making for a fence corner, continue alongside the fence, climb a stile and cross a drive by the gate of the Powick Sewage Treatment Works. Keep ahead across the next field, heading towards a footpath sign on the far side, and turn right along an enclosed track. Be-fore reaching a cottage, turn right to cross a footbridge over a ditch and turn left along the left edge of two fields, climbing a stile and keeping parallel to the track. Go through a gap in the corner of the second field, bear right across the next field and climb a stile onto a road. Opposite is the entrance to Stanbrook Abbey [C]. Turn left into Callow End and where the road curves right in front of a triangular green, bear left along Lower Ferry Lane. At a public footpath sign, turn right through a kissing gate, walk along a path, by a brook on the right, go through another kiss-ing gate and keep ahead to a road. Turn right back to the main road and take the tarmac drive opposite, passing the Old Bush pub. Climb a stile

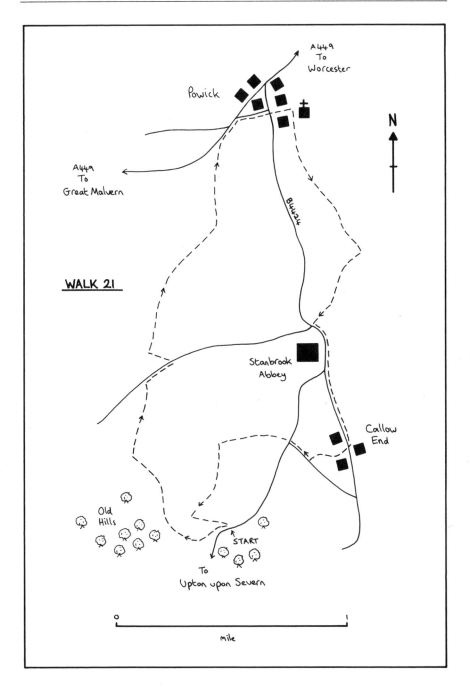

N

A449
To
Worcester

Powick

A449
To
Great Malvern

B4424

WALK 21

Stanbrook
Abbey

Callow
End

Old
Hills

START

To
Upton upon Severn

0   1

mile

and walk along a track, climbing two more stiles before continuing along a left field edge. Climb another stile but before reaching the end of the next field, turn left through a gate and keep along the left edge of a field.

Climb two more stiles – crossing a track in between – head gently uphill along the left edge of a field and climb a stile in the corner. Keep ahead, passing to the right of a house, and pick up a track which bends left to a T-junction. Turn left and the track bends right to return to the start.

Features of Interest

A. Although rising to a modest height of only 230 feet (70m), the smooth, grassy slopes of the Old Hills provide outstanding and extensive views over the Worcestershire countryside. These include the switchback ridge of the Malverns, Bredon Hill and – further away – the Abberley and Clent hills. A nearer landmark is the tower of Worcester Cathedral.

B. The medieval church at Powick, which dates mainly from the 12th and 13th centuries, stands in a commanding position on a low ridge near where the Teme flows into the Severn a few miles downstream from Worcester. It is quite a large and imposing building, with a west tower and transepts at the east end.

C. A Benedictine nunnery was founded here in 1838. The buildings, designed by E.W. Pugin in a red brick Gothic style, were erected in the late 19th century.

22. Great Malvern and the Worcestershire Beacon

Start: Great Malvern, in town centre at the top of Church Street between the priory and tourist information centre – grid reference 775459

Distance: 2½ miles (4km)

Category: Fairly strenuous

Parking: Great Malvern

Refreshments: Pubs and cafés at Great Malvern, café at St Ann's Well

Terrain: Mostly over open hilltop and through woodland, some steep climbs and descents

OS Maps: Landranger 150, Explorer 190

Public Transport: Buses from Worcester, Ledbury and Hereford; trains from Birmingham, Worcester, Ledbury and Hereford

Explore & Discover

Despite its brief length, this walk involves a stiff climb to the highest point on the Malverns – and indeed in the whole of Worcestershire – followed by quite a steep descent. The climb onto the Malvern ridge and up to the Worcestershire Beacon rewards you with outstanding and extensive views and it is best to choose a fine, clear day in order to see them at their best. Throughout the walk there are plenty of seats and benches to enable you to do this in comfort. Additional interest is provided by Great Malvern Priory at the start and St Ann's Well towards the end. There are numerous paths and tracks on the hills and the route directions need to be followed carefully, although the regular marker stones and circular direction indicators erected by the Malvern Hills Conservators are an invaluable aid to successful route finding.

Route Directions

Facing the hills and Belle Vue Terrace, [A] turn right. Turn left into St Ann's Road, signposted to Worcestershire Beacon, and head steeply up through the trees. The road later becomes a tarmac drive and where this bends sharply left, keep ahead along a steadily ascending track, in the

West Malvern and Beacon direction. At a fork, take the left-hand narrower path to emerge onto the open grassy slopes of the Malvern ridge and at a crossroads, turn left onto a well-surfaced track. Keep ahead at the first crossroads to reach a circular stone direction indicator at the second crossroads. From here take the narrower path ahead which climbs more steeply, curving right on joining a track and continuing steadily up to the summit where you turn sharply left to the trig point and viewfinder. The views are magnificent, extending across Herefordshire to the Black Mountains of South Wales and over the Vale of Severn to Bredon Hill and the line of the Cotswolds [B].

At the trig point turn right to continue along the ridge in the same direction as before and the path descends into a dip to meet a well-surfaced track. Turn sharp left along it but after about 20 yards (18m), bear right onto a narrow path which contours across the hillside below the Beacon. At a fork, take the right-hand lower path which descends steeply to a junction and turn half-right along a path which continues downhill to join another path. Bear left along it across gorse, bracken and rough grass – above a steep valley on the right – and the path continues to contour across the hillside to reach a bench with a glorious view over Great Malvern below.

At a fork by this bench, continue along the right-hand lower path which curves around the head of a valley to enter trees and reach a T-junction. Turn right, at the next T-junction turn right again to St Ann's Well and turn left down steps beside the well [C]. Continue along

St Ann's Well

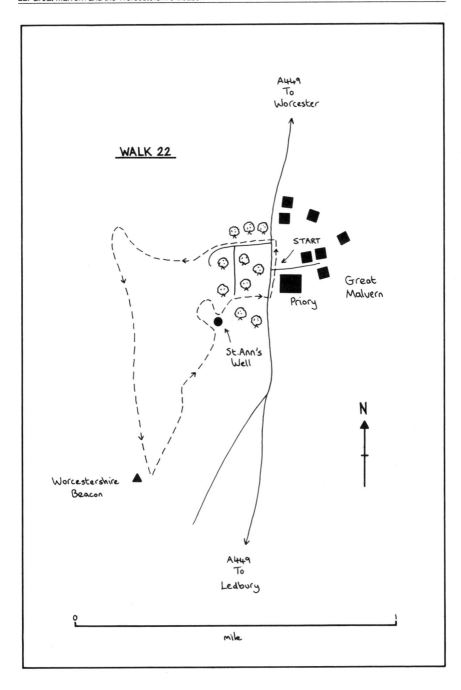

WALK 22

A449
To
Worcester

START

Great
Malvern

Priory

St.Ann's
Well

Worcestershire
Beacon

N

A449
To
Ledbury

0   1

mile

a tarmac track which winds quite steeply downhill to a road. Turn sharp right and at the fork immediately ahead, take the left-hand tarmac drive. Descend steps to the left of the gates to a large house, turning left and continuing down into Rose Bank Gardens and through gates onto the road opposite Great Malvern Priory. Turn left to the start.

Features of Interest

A. Great Malvern is the largest of the group of widely scattered settlements nestling around the base and on the lower slopes of the hills. It was originally a small village huddled around its medieval priory but grew rapidly from the middle of the 18th century onwards when it became famous for its spring water. Its heyday as a fashionable spa was in the Victorian and Edwardian eras and many fine and elegant buildings survive from that period. Even today the town retains a pleasantly old fashioned and genteel atmosphere. Externally Great Malvern Priory is a predominantly 15th-century building with an imposing Perpendicular central tower but immediately on entering the church, the scene is dominated by the Norman nave. It was founded as a Benedictine priory in 1085 and dissolved by Henry VIII in the 1530s. The 15th-century stained glass is amongst the finest in the country.

B. Rising abruptly above the surrounding countryside, the Malvern Hills resemble a mini-mountain range and are amongst the most popular walking areas in the Midlands. The views from the ridge path are magnificent, extending over a huge swathe of the country from the edge of Birmingham to the mountains of South Wales. At 1395 feet (425m), the Worcestershire Beacon is the highest point on the hills. One of the great advantages of the Malverns is that there are miles of paths and tracks and almost unlimited freedom to roam. This is mainly thanks to the work of the Malverns Hills Conservators who have been responsible for maintaining the area for public enjoyment and recreation since 1884, one of the earliest conservation bodies in Britain.

C. It was in the 18th century that visitors started coming here to take the waters and the main building was erected around 1815 to cater for the ever growing numbers. Nowadays it is a café.

---

23. Little Malvern and the British Camp

Start/Parking: British Camp car park, off A449 on Worcestershire-Herefordshire border – grid reference 764404

Distance: 4½ miles (7.2km)

Category: Fairly strenuous

Refreshments: Malvern Hills Hotel and kiosk at start

Terrain: Some climbing – with a steep ascent and descent towards the end – but generally clear and well-surfaced paths all the way

OS Maps: Landranger 150, Explorer 190

Public Transport: Buses from Great Malvern, Worcester and Birmingham only on summer Sundays and Bank Holidays

---

Explore & Discover

There can be few hill and woodland walks of such modest length anywhere in the country that provide more outstanding views. These encompass the Malvern ridge, Herefordshire, the Black Mountains, Vale of Severn, Bredon Hill and the western escarpment of the Cotswolds. Historic interest is centred on the grave of Sir Edward Elgar, Little Malvern Priory and Court and the prehistoric hillfort of the British Camp. The walk involves quite a lot of climbing and, as on Walk 22, there are some marker stones and circular stone direction indicators, erected by the Malvern Hills Conservators, to aid route finding.

Route Directions

Start by walking along the road opposite the car park, signposted to West Malvern, and after passing the drive of the Malvern Hills Hotel, bear right onto a path. At a fork immediately in front, take the right-hand upper path which continues through a belt of trees onto the top of a small hill. To the left is a fine view looking along the Malvern ridge [A]. The path enters woodland and at at a fork, take the right-hand path through the trees which descends and goes round a very sharp left bend. Keep ahead along this delightful wooded path which contours across the hillside, later emerging into more open country. To the right are superb views, with Little Malvern Court and Priory below. At a crossroads, turn right downhill through woodland once more to a road and turn sharp right down to the main road. Turn right again into Little Malvern, passing St Wulstan's Roman Catholic church on the left. Elgar's grave is in the churchyard [B]. The road bears left, in the Upton direction, bends left and heads downhill to Little Malvern Court [C] and Priory [D]. Just before reaching the Court, turn right onto a tarmac track and keep along it to a farm. Continue past the farm on what is now a rough track and after going through a gate, bear right onto a grassy track which heads uphill along the right edge of a field, curving right to a gate. Go through, keep ahead across a field and at a hedge corner, bear right across grass to pick up a path that continues steeply uphill through woodland. At a T-junction, turn right onto a downhill path which, after passing to the right of a house, continues as a track, bearing left to a junction. Turn sharp right along an uphill track, keep ahead at a crossroads, in the Giant's Cave and British Camp direction, and continue up to a fork. Here take the left-hand path and at the next fork, continue along the left-hand lower path, passing the Giant's or Clutter's Cave [E]. Continue past the cave into more open country to reach a circular stone indicator and turn left, in the British Camp direction.

Head steeply uphill along a stone path, continue across grass and descend slightly to pick up a clear, broad, well-surfaced path which heads up over the earthworks of the British Camp [F]. The views from here are magnificent. At the top, descend steps and continue along a well-surfaced path which descends more steps, noting where you turn right down a long flight of steps. At the bottom the path curves left down to the car park.

Features of Interest

A. For details of the Malvern Hills, see Walk 22

B. Elgar was buried here next to his wife in February 1934, on the slopes of his beloved Malverns and overlooking the Vale of Severn.

C. The house is mostly Elizabethan, with 19th-century additions, but also incorporates the Prior's Hall from the medieval priory. From the

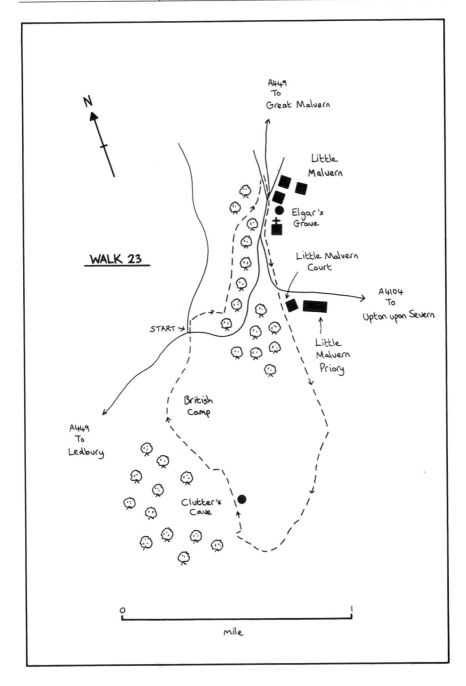

N

A449
To
Great Malvern

Little
Malvern

Elgar's
Grave

Little Malvern
Court

A4104
To
Upton upon Severn

WALK 23

START →

Little
Malvern
Priory

British
Camp

A449
To
Ledbury

Clutter's
Cave

0   1
mile

attractive gardens there are fine views of the Malverns and across the Vale of Severn.

D. The Benedictine priory at Little Malvern was one of the smallest in the country and never had more than around a dozen monks. Founded in the 12th century, the remains comprise just the east end and tower of the church, built in the 15th century.

E. There are all sorts of stories and legends about the alleged occupant of this cave but it is certainly not large enough to have housed a giant.

F. The extensive and impressive earthworks of the British Camp occupy the Herefordshire Beacon, at 1114 feet (340m) one of the highest summits on the Malverns and an excellent vantage point. It is one of the largest Iron Age hillforts in the country, more than 30 acres in area and with a circumference of over a mile. A Norman castle was later built in the centre of the fort, adding to the complexity of the surviving earthworks.

24. Upton upon Severn and Earl's Croome

Start/Parking: Upton upon Severn, Hanley Road car park – grid reference 852407

Distance: 5 miles (8km)

Category: Easy

Refreshments: Pubs and cafés at Upton upon Severn, Yorkshire Grey just before Earl's Croome

Terrain: Mainly flat walk across fields and riverside meadows

OS Maps: Landranger 150, Explorer 190

Public Transport: Buses from Worcester, Tewkesbury and Gloucester

Explore & Discover

From the bustle of the riverside town of Upton upon Severn, the route heads across fields to the quiet and off the beaten track village of Earl's Croome. From there you continue down to the banks of the River Severn and the remainder of the walk is a relaxing stroll across riverside meadows, following the Severn Way back to Upton. At many points on the route, there are fine views across the surrounding flat landscape to the Malverns and Bredon Hill.

Route Directions

Start by turning right along the road towards the distinctive 'Pepperpot'. The town centre of Upton is ahead [A] but the route turns left to cross the bridge over the River Severn. At a public footpath sign, descend to climb a stile, bear left and head across a meadow, making for a stile to the right of a gate where you cross a ditch. After climbing the stile, keep ahead in the same direction, passing through a hedge gap where you cross another ditch. Continue across the meadow, over another ditch, and in the far corner cross a footbridge over one more ditch. Head uphill across a field, keeping to the right of a pond and farm buildings, cross a tarmac drive, keep ahead – passing another small pond –

Looking across the River Severn to the village of Hanley Castle

and bear slightly right along the left edge of a field to go through a kissing gate in the corner. Continue gently uphill along the left edge of the
next field, climb two stiles in quick succession and walk across a field
to a stile on the far side. After climbing that, keep ahead along a track,
pass through farm buildings and go through a gate onto the A38. At a
public footpath sign to Earl's Croome almost opposite – just to the left of
the entrance to the drive to Earl's Croome Court – climb a stile and follow the direction of the yellow waymark across a field, making for a
stile on the far side about 50 yards (46m) to the left of the field corner.
Climb it, continue across the next field, climb a stile in the corner, turn
right along the right field edge and climb another stile onto a lane. Earl's
Croome church is just to the right [B]. The route continues to the left
and where the lane curves right, turn left and at a public footpath sign,
turn right along a paved enclosed path beside bungalows. Follow the
path to the right and turn left over a stile. Turn half-left and head diagonally across a field, skirting a circular pond and continuing in the same
direction to go through a hedge gap on the far side. Continue in the same
direction, skirting a hedge corner, on to the far right-hand corner of the
field where you go through a gate – or climb a stile – on to the A38 again.

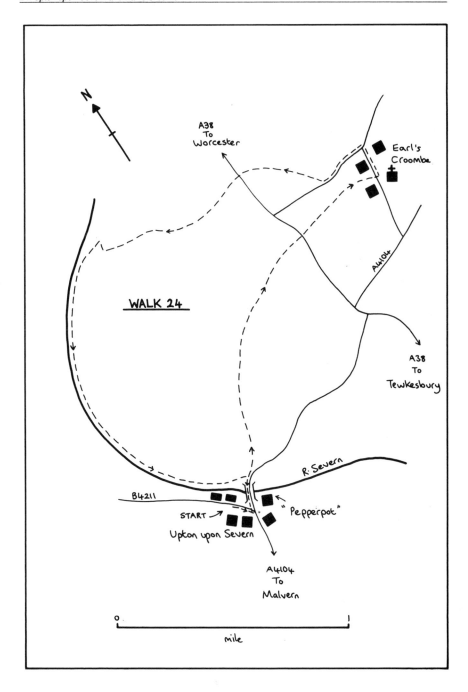

Turn left and at a public bridleway sign to River – by Earl's Croome Nursery and Garden Centre – turn right along a track. Where the track turns left, keep ahead along a hedge- and tree-lined path to a gate. Go through, walk along the left edge of a field and in the bottom corner, look out for a hedge gap where you go through a gate onto a track. Turn right to the river, turn left along the riverbank – here joining the Severn Way – and follow it along the edge of meadows, negotiating several stiles and gates, back to Upton upon Severn. Just before Upton Bridge, bear left onto a track, go through a gate and pass under the road. Turn sharp right along a tarmac path up to the road and turn left over the bridge to return to the start.

Features of Interest

A. Although the present bridge is modern, there has been a crossing on this site – the only crossing of the River Severn between Worcester and Tewkesbury – for centuries, the main reason for Upton's existence and its previous importance as a river port. The major landmark in this pleasant little town is the distinctive 18th-century cupola that caps the medieval church tower, nicknamed 'The Pepperpot'. Only the tower is left – now used as a heritage centre – as the rest of the church was destroyed during a minor conflict between Cromwell's troops and Royalist forces in 1651 just before the Battle of Worcester.

B. The medieval church at Earl's Croome is a short building with a sturdy-looking west tower. The latter was built in the 19th century in a neo-Norman style to harmonise with the rest of the church. .

25. Pershore and Wick

Start/Parking: Pershore Bridges Picnic Place, off A44 half a mile (0.8km) south of Pershore – grid reference 952451

Distance: The full walk is 4 miles (6.4km), the shorter version – which omits the extension into Pershore – is 3 miles (4.8km)

Category: Easy

Refreshments: Pubs and cafés at Pershore

Terrain: Flat walking mainly on clear paths, tracks and narrow lanes

OS Maps: Landranger 150, Explorer 190

Public Transport: Buses from Evesham and Worcester

Explore & Discover

The shorter version of the route is an easy circuit of the flat country that lies to the east and south of the River Avon between Pershore and the

Pershore Bridge

village of Wick. From several points, there are expansive views across the fields to the tower of Pershore Abbey and the line of the Malverns. The full walk has the added interest of a visit to Pershore town centre, noted for its partially ruined medieval abbey and fine Georgian architecture.

Route Directions

At a public footpath sign to Wick just in front of the Old Bridge, [A] turn right onto a tarmac path. Go through a gate, follow the path across a meadow, go through another gate on the far side and continue along an enclosed path to a lane. Turn right and the lane curves left through the small village of Wick [B]. Keep ahead to see the church but the route turns left along School Lane. The lane peters out into a rough track which continues across fields and bears right to a lane. Turn left along this narrow lane – in front the houses of Wyre Piddle can be seen on the other side of the Avon – and at a public footpath sign, turn left along a track. Pass between a brick bungalow on the left and barns on the right and keep ahead across a field, joining a wire fence on the right. In the field corner climb two stiles in quick succession, continue along the left edge of a field, by a ditch and line of trees on the left, cross a footbridge and keep ahead across the next field – by a hedge on the left for most of the way – to a track and waymarked post on the far side. Bear left, cross a track and make for a stile just to the left of a fence corner. After climbing it, continue in the same direction to the end of a lane and bear left along it back into Wick. At a public footpath sign on the edge of the village, turn right onto a tarmac path, here picking up the outward route, and retrace your steps to the start.

For the short detour into Pershore, cross the Old Bridge and turn right along the main road into the town. Turn left into Broad Street and at a T-junction, turn right to the abbey [C]. From the abbey, walk along Church Street back to the main road and turn right to return to the start.

Features of Interest

A. For many centuries the medieval Old Bridge was the only crossing point over the River Avon.

B. Wick is a delightful village, a mixture of old and new with several black and white thatched cottages. The tiny church, with a simple

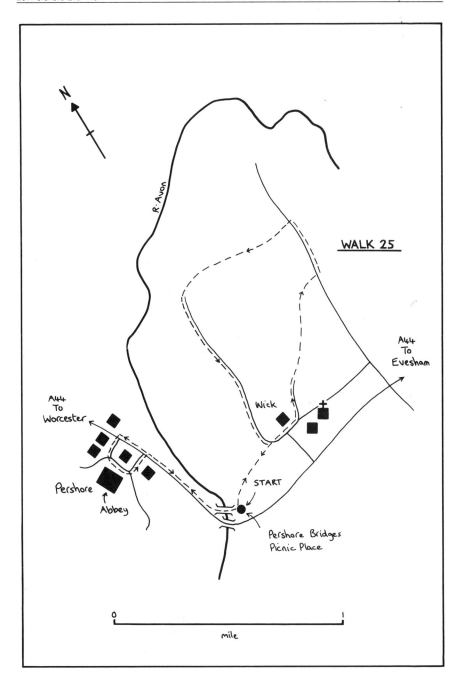

N

R. Avon

WALK 25

A44
To
Evesham

A44
To
Worcester

Wick

Pershore

Abbey

START

Pershore Bridges
Picnic Place

0   1

mile

bellcote at the west end, is of Norman origin but was heavily restored in the 19th century. In the field next to the church is part of an ancient cross.

C. Pershore Abbey was founded in 689 and dissolved by Henry VIII and Thomas Cromwell in 1539. Unusually it is the east end – the monastic half of the church – that has survived the destruction of the Reformation as the local parish church instead of the nave. The remains comprise the Norman south transept, superb 13th-century presbytery and imposing 14th-century tower, the latter rebuilt after a disastrous fire in 1288. Just across the road is the medieval church of St Andrew and in the town centre – especially along the main road – there are some fine Georgian houses.

26. Bredon Hill

Start/Parking: Elmley Castle Picnic Place, about 200 yards (183m) east of the village centre – grid reference 984411

Distance: 8 miles (12.9km)

Category: Moderate

Refreshments: Elizabeth Queen of England and Old Mill Inn at Elmley Castle

Terrain: Relatively easy ascents and descents of Bredon Hill, finishing with a flat walk along tracks and field paths at the base

OS Maps: Landranger 150, Explorer 190

Public Transport: Occasional buses from Pershore

Explore & Discover

The detached and distinctive outline of Bredon Hill rises to a height of 980 feet (299m) above the Vale of Evesham. It is really an outlying hill of the Cotswolds and, from its summit, the views across to the main Cotswold range and over the vale to the line of the Malverns, with the winding River Avon and numerous village church towers seen below, are particularly memorable. Both the ascent and descent are gradual and relatively easy and an added bonus is the two picturesque villages of Elmley Castle and Great Comberton nestling at the foot of the hill. It is definitely worth saving this delightful walk for a fine day in order to enjoy the extensive views at their best.

Route Directions

Turn right along the lane away from the village and turn right again, at a public bridleway sign, to join the Wychavon Way and begin the gradual ascent of Bredon Hill. Walk along the left edge of a field, keep ahead through trees in the field corner, go through a gate and along a wide tree-lined track to a waymarked post. Bear right across a plank footbridge, uphill between trees and along a track, by a hedge and line of trees on the right, to a gate. Go through, keep ahead uphill and in front of a gate. Turn first left, then right and continue up through the trees, going through a gate to emerge onto the open hilltop. Keep ahead along a fence-lined track, by the left edge of woodland. Go through a gate at the corner of the wood (Long Plantation) and continue across the hill, initially by a wire fence on the left and later alongside a wall on the right. To the left are the extensive earthworks of a prehistoric fort. The path bends left to pass a large stone (Banbury Stone) and a tower which, together with the fort, occupy the summit of Bredon Hill [A]. Continue past the tower, go through two gates and enter woodland after the second one. Take the broad path through the trees and at a public footpath sign, turn right down to a metal stile to begin the descent to Great Comberton. Climb the stile, head downhill to climb another and continue downhill across a field. Make for a waymarked post near the bottom end and continue beyond that to a stile. Climb it and, at the T-junction ahead, turn left along a track. After climbing two more stiles, bear left off the track and head across a field towards a large house (Woolas Hall). Climb a stile to the right of it, turn right alongside a wire fence on the right, cross the track that you were previously walking along and go through a gate.

Continue along a track, climbing another stile. After the track peters out, keep straight ahead to a public footpath sign. Here turn left to pass through a line of trees and continue along the right field edge to a stile. Climb it, continue downhill and, after the next stile, bear slightly right to keep along the right edge of a field, by a small brook on the right, and climb a stile onto a lane. Turn right uphill and at a T-junction, keep ahead along an enclosed path towards Great Comberton church [B]. Go through a kissing gate into the churchyard, pass to the left of the church and go through a gate onto a lane in the village. Turn left. At a 'No Through Road' sign turn right along a lane (Russell Street) and, where the lane peters out, keep ahead along a track slightly above ditches on both sides. After the track bears slightly left to pass through a gap, walk along the right edge of a field, bearing right and then left and continuing gently uphill, by a low embankment on the right. Descend to pass through another hedge gap and keep ahead along an enclosed path – likely to be muddy – to a T-junction. Turn right along an enclosed track and just after emerging from the trees, turn left over a stile and walk along the left edge of a field to climb a stile in the corner. Cross a plank footbridge, immediately climb a stile and continue along the right edge of a field. Climb another stile, keep ahead in the same direction across the next field, climb a stile on the far side and keep along the right edge of a field. Turn right through a gate in the corner, keep along a left field edge, climb a stile and turn left along the left field edge to another stile.

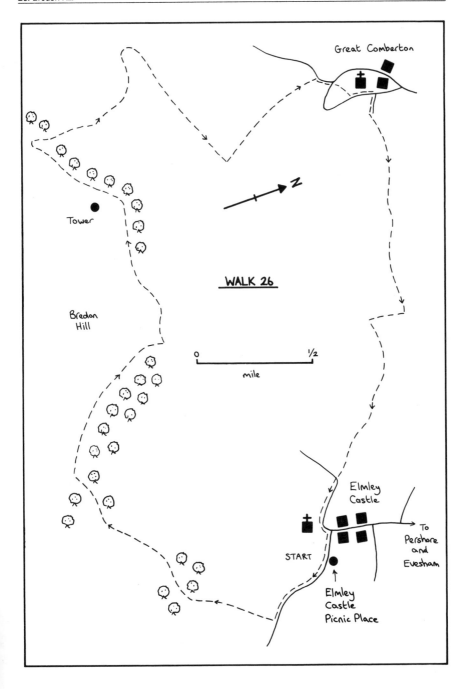

Great Comberton

Z

Tower

WALK 26

Bredon
Hill

0   ½
            mile

Elmley
Castle

To
Pershore
and
Evesham

START

Elmley
Castle
Picnic Place

Elmley Castle

Climb that and another and continue along the left field edge towards a farm. Pass through the farmyard, keep to the left of a barn and turn right around the end of it to a stile. After climbing it, keep ahead along a path to a lane and turn left into Elmley Castle [C]. In the village centre, turn left and immediately right to return to the start.

Features of Interest

A. Bredon Hill, an outlier of the Cotswolds, has been immortalised in these words by Worcestershire-born A.E. Housman: 'In summertime on Bredon the bells they sound so clear; Round both the shires they ring them in steeples far and near, A happy noise to hear.' The views from the top, looking out across the Vale of Evesham to the outline of the Clee and Malvern hills on the horizon, are magnificent and several church towers can be seen below, including that of Pershore Abbey. The 18th-century tower that occupies the summit, known as Parsons Folly, stands within the earthworks of an Iron Age fort.

B. Thatched and half-timbered cottages, presided over by the tower of the medieval church, create a delightful scene at the quiet and secluded village of Great Comberton.

C. Elmley Castle is another exceptionally attractive village, with black and white cottages lining the main street and a stream running beside it. Of the castle of the powerful Despenser family, from which the village gets its name, there is virtually no trace. The handsome medieval church, which has a Norman chancel and a 13th-century tower, lies in an attractive position at the south end of the village below Bredon Hill.

27. Around Evesham

Start: Evesham, Market Place – grid reference 037437

Distance: 3½ miles (5.6km)

Category: Easy

Parking: Evesham

Refreshments: Pubs and cafés at Evesham

Terrain: Mainly riverside meadows

OS Maps: Landranger 150, Explorer 205

Public transport: Evesham is served by buses from Worcester, Stratford-upon-Avon, Redditch, Birmingham, Tewkesbury and Cheltenham, and by trains from Worcester and Oxford.

Explore & Discover

Like Durham and Shrewsbury, Evesham sits within a horseshoe bend of a river. Apart from a short stretch of about three-quarters of a mile (1.2km) across the 'neck' of the horseshoe, the walk mostly follows the banks of the Avon around this bend. Allow plenty of time to explore the town, with its interesting monastic remains and attractive riverside parks and meadows.

Route Directions

With your back to the entrance to Abbey Gates Shopping Centre, turn left and pass under the Abbey Gateway into the Abbey Churchyard [A]. Follow the path to the left to pass under the Bell Tower and keep ahead through Abbey Park to descend to the River Avon.

Turn right along the tree-lined riverside promenade, pass under a road bridge and continue beside the Avon, following the curve of the river to the right. To the left the little River Isbourne can be seen flowing into the Avon, and over to the right there are pleasant views across fields to the town, dominated by the Bell Tower of the former abbey. Continue past the Hampton Ferry, [B] first along the edge of more river-side meadows, then along a tarmac drive beside a cricket ground and

Almonry, Evesham

bowling green, and finally alongside a sports field. After crossing a ditch – and about half-way along the edge of the sports field – turn right away from the river and keep beside a ditch. In the field corner, go through a fence gap and walk gently uphll along a hedge-lined path. The path widens into a track which continues to a tarmac drive on the edge of an industrial estate. Turn right to a road, keep along it and take the first road on the left to a T-junction at the top end of Evesham High Street. Turn left and just before the station, turn right into St Mary's Road. Where the road ends, keep ahead down an enclosed path, parallel to the railway line, to reach a track in front of Evesham United football ground. Turn right – the track later becomes a road – and at a wall corner, turn left down a track towards the river and turn right onto a path. Go through a kissing gate, continue beside the Avon – diverting briefly to cross a slipway – and the path bears right away from the river to a lane. Turn left to a road junction and bear left to a T-junction to the right of Workman Bridge. Turn right along pedestrianised Bridge Street to return to the Market Place.

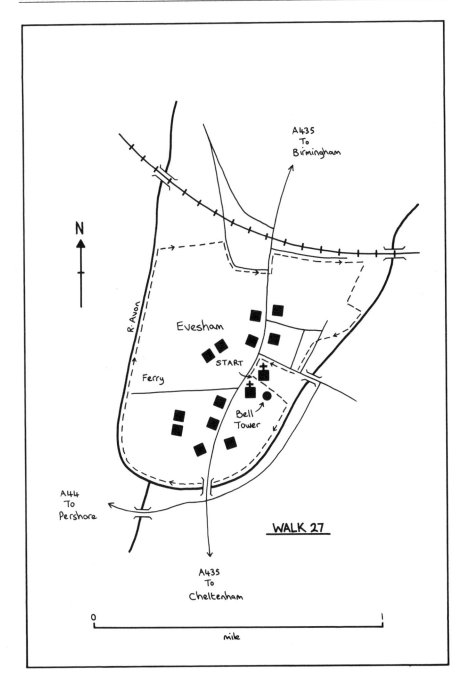

N

A435
To
Birmingham

R. Avon

Evesham

START

Ferry

Bell
Tower

A44
To
Pershore

WALK 27

A435
To
Cheltenham

0   1

mile

Features of Interest

A. Its attractive location, riverside parks and meadows, good communications and an abundance of refreshment places has long made Evesham a favourite weekend destination for Midlanders. The town originally grew up around its powerful and wealthy Benedictine abbey, which was founded in 714. Only fragments of this remain, apart from the imposing detached Bell Tower, 110 feet high and built in the early 16th century by the last abbot only a few years before the abbey was dissolved. Other monastic survivals are the Gateway and 14th-century Almonry. The latter is now a heritage and tourist information centre.

The Abbey Gateway is in one corner of the spacious Market Place which possesses two imposing buildings, the Town Hall and Round House. The latter, recently restored, is a fine example of a 15th-century timber-framed merchant's house. Unusually there are two adjacent medieval churches within the precincts of the former abbey. One theory is that All Saints was used by the local people and St Lawrence's was built for pilgrims to the abbey. Both are impressive buildings with spires above their west towers and fine examples of fan vaulting inside.

B. The Hampton Ferry claims to be the world's only rope-drawn ferry. It operates during the summer months and links Evesham with Hampton.

28. Harvington and the Lenches

Start: Harvington, by the church – grid reference 056488

Distance: 8½ miles (13.7km)

Category: Moderate

Parking: Roadside parking in Harvington

Refreshments: Coach and Horses and Golden Cross at Harvington

Terrain: Undulating route along tracks and field paths

OS Maps: Landranger 150, Explorer 205

Public transport: Infrequent bus service between Evesham and Bidford-on-Avon

Atch Lench

Explore & Discover

The Lenches are a group of five villages and hamlets enclosed within low hills on the northern edge of the Vale of Evesham. Starting from the larger village of Harvington, the walk links three of these. There is some gentle climbing and from many points, there are extensive views across the vale. Much of the last part of the route is through some of the orchards for which the Vale of Evesham is renowned and which inevitably look their best at blossom time.

Route Directions

Begin by facing the church and turning right [A]. Where the road curves left, turn right and at a public footpath sign, turn left along Finch Lane. The lane bends right and at a fork, take the right-hand tarmac track. Where this ends, keep ahead along an enclosed path and turn right onto a track. Turn left at a T-junction and follow the track to the right which eventually emerges onto a road almost opposite the Golden Cross. Turn left to a crossroads, turn right and at a public footpath sign, turn left onto a track across fields. The track bears slightly left towards a farm. About 100 yards (91m) after passing to the right of a ruined cottage, bear slightly right off the broad track and continue along a faint path which runs in a straight line across fields, making for the left edge of a hedge which can be seen in the distance. On reaching this hedge, join a track along its right edge and after the track bends left, keep ahead – there is a waymarked post here – towards a belt of trees. The path curves left through the trees, bears right and continues along a left field edge. Where the hedge ends, go round left and right curves and head uphill, bearing left at the top on joining another track. Follow the track to the left to emerge onto a lane in Atch Lench [B]. Turn right through this lovely hamlet and where the lane bends right, keep ahead over a stile and head downhill across a field to cross a footbridge over a brook. Climb a stile, walk gently uphill, in the top right-hand field corner negotiate first a stile and then a gate and continue in the same direction across the next field to climb another stile onto a track. The route continues to the left but in order to take a look at Church Lench – well worth a brief diversion – turn right along a tarmac drive, turn left along Main Street and by the church, turn left in the Lenchwick and Evesham direction. At a public footpath sign, turn left onto a tarmac drive, bear slightly left through a kissing gate and continue along a narrow,

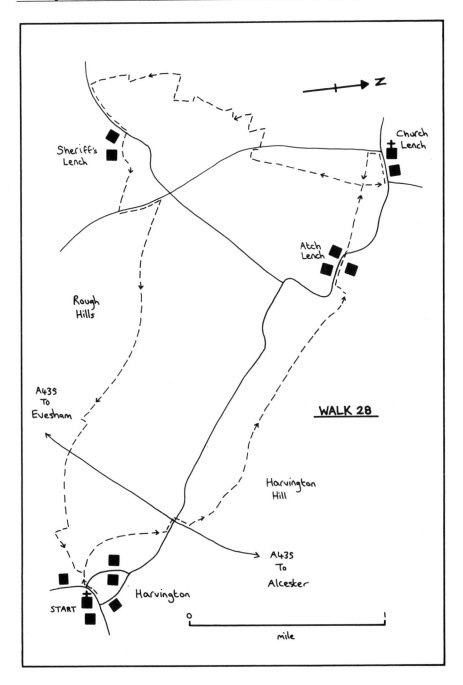

Z

Church
Lench

Sheriff's
Lench

Atch
Lench

Rough
Hills

A435
To
Evesham

WALK 28

Harvington
Hill

A435
To
Alcester

Harvington

START

0   1

mile

hedge-lined path to a stile. Climb it, walk along the left field edge and in the corner, keep ahead along a track to a T-junction, here rejoining the previous route.

Turn right along a straight track and follow it – over two stiles and later along the right edge of an orchard – as far as a tarmac track. The next part of the walk is on the well-waymarked Wychavon Way. Turn right along the track to a lane, turn right again and at a public footpath sign, turn left over a stile and walk along the right edge of a field. Turn left in the corner and continue by the right field edge around a series of right angle bends as far as a footbridge over a ditch. After crossing it, turn left to continue along the left edge of fields until joining a track by a hedge gap.

Turn right along the track and at the next Wychavon Way sign, turn left off it and walk along the right field edge. Turn right at a wide hedge gap, turn left to pass through another hedge gap and continue by the left edge of a field to a lane. Turn left, follow the lane around a left bend into the hamlet of Sheriff's Lench and at the next left bend, turn right onto a tarmac drive. Where this drive turns right, keep ahead along a track which bears left along the left edge of an orchard. At the corner of the orchard, turn right onto a path which continues along its left edge to a lane. Turn left and after a quarter of a mile (0.4km), turn right beside a gate and walk along a track towards a barn. Keep straight ahead across a field and on the far side, continue through a narrow belt of trees and bushes and on across the next field to pass through a waymarked hedge gap. Head gently uphill in a straight line across the next field and at a waymarked post on the brow, bear slightly left and continue across the field, looking out for a hedge gap on the far side just to the right of the last of a line of widely spaced trees.

Go through the gap, head downhill – making for an obvious hedge gap and beyond that a broad grassy path – and continue first along this path and then along the left edge of a field. There are fine views over the vale at this point, with the spire of Harvington church clearly visible. Go through a gap in the corner, keep ahead along an enclosed track and continue through orchards. The track bends first to the left and then to the right and continues through the orchards and along a tarmac drive to a road. Turn left and at a public footpath sign, turn right along a track between houses which continues across more orchards. Follow this track around two right and left bends and after the last of these, it descends to a footbridge over Harvington Brook. Continue uphill along a narrow enclosed path, turn left over a stile and walk along a track which bears right and becomes a lane. Here you pick up the outward route and retrace your steps to Harvington church.

Features of Interest

A. Like most villages in the Vale of Evesham, Harvington has its fair share of attractive, black and white cottages. The medieval church has a fine Norman tower, with a spire added in 1855. The latter is a landmark for much of the second half of the walk.

B. Atch Lench has some beautiful thatched and half-timbered cottages and there are more of them a little further on in the hilltop village of Church Lench. Here the medieval church commands fine views over the vale.

29. Cleeve Prior, the Littletons and Cleeve Hill

Start: Cleeve Prior, at triangular green by Memorial Hall and church – grid reference 087494

Distance: 5½ miles (8.9km)

Category: Moderate

Parking: Roadside parking at Cleeve Prior

Refreshments: Kings Arms at Cleeve Prior, Ivy Inn at North Littleton, King Edward VII at South Littleton

Terrain: Apart from a brief climb onto a low ridge, this is an almost entirely flat walk across fields and along a ridge top path

OS Maps: Landranger 150, Explorer 205

Public transport: Buses from Birmingham, Redditch and Evesham

Explore & Discover

The first half of the route is mainly across fields from Cleeve Prior, passing through the adjacent villages of North, Middle and South Littleton. A brief and easy climb onto a low ridge above the River Avon is followed by a superb 2-mile (3.2km) ridge top walk, from which there are grand views across the wide expanses of the Vale of Evesham to the line of the Cotswolds, Bredon Hill and the Malverns. There are medieval churches at Cleeve Prior, Middle Littleton and South Littleton, and a tithe barn next to the church at Middle Littleton.

Route Directions

With your back to the green, [A] take the hedge-lined track opposite (Quarry Lane), signposted to Littleton, which bends left and continues in a straight line across fields, later narrowing to a path. After following the field edge to the right, turn left to cross a footbridge over a ditch and continue - again in a straight line - along the right edge of fields to a stile. Climb it and keep ahead to eventually climb a stile onto a lane. Turn left into North Littleton and just before reaching a small green in front of the

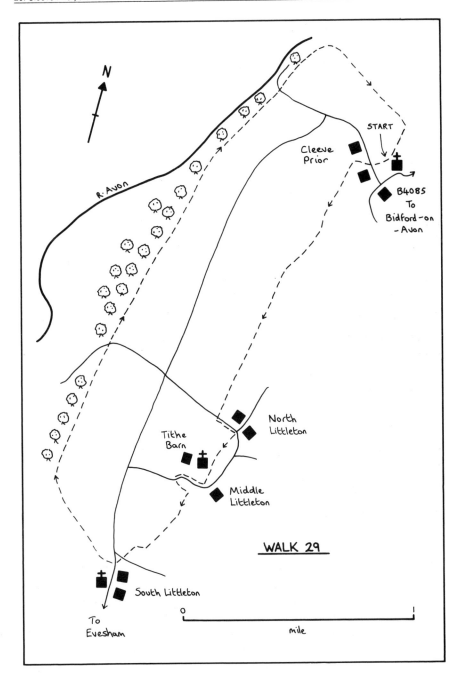

N

R. Avon

Cleeve
Prior

START

B4085
To
Bidford-on
-Avon

North
Littleton

Tithe
Barn

Middle
Littleton

WALK 29

South Littleton

To
Evesham

0 ——————————— 1

mile

Ivy Inn, turn right along a path between houses. Continue across two fields in the direction of Middle Littleton church and after climbing a stile on the far side of the second field, keep ahead to go through a gate into the churchyard. Keeping to the left of the church, go through a kissing gate and turn right along a lane [B]. At a left bend, turn right for the Tithe Barn. Otherwise follow the lane around the bend and at a right bend, turn left through a gate and walk along a track through a farm to a stile. Climb it, keep ahead, turn right through a kissing gate and walk along an enclosed path to a road. Turn left, follow the road around a right bend and at a public footpath sign, bear left along a tarmac track and go through a kissing gate into a field. Bear slightly right, making for a kissing gate in a hedge on the far side, go through the gate and continue along an enclosed path which curves left to emerge onto a lane in South Littleton. Keep ahead to a road, bear left and turn right along Church Lane, passing to the right of the church. Where the lane ends, keep ahead, at a public bridleway sign to Cleeve Prior, along the drive to Church Farm and continue gently uphill along a track. Take the right-hand track at a fork and continue up to the top of a low ridge. Just before the brow, turn right onto a broad track and at the three-way fork

Approaching Middle Littleton

immediately in front, take the left-hand path, passing by a blue-waymarked post. For the next 2 miles (3.2km), you follow a splendid ridge path along the top of Cleeve Hill. Initially there are fine open views to the left across the wide expanses of the Vale of Evesham to Bredon Hill and the Malverns on the horizon, with the River Avon winding below. Later - after crossing a road - the path becomes enclosed between trees and hedges but gaps on both sides reveal more grand views. After crossing a second road - a narrow lane - keep ahead along a tarmac track above the river as far as a gate just beyond a house on the left. Go through it and immediately turn right onto a grassy path across fields.

Keep ahead at a crossroads of tracks and at a T-junction, climb the stile in front and walk along the right edge of a field. Turn right over a stile, turn left to continue along the left field edge, climb a stile and keep along the left edge of the next field. Climb another stile in the corner, turn right along the right edge of a field, cross a footbridge and continue across the next field towards Cleeve Prior church. Climb a stile on the far side, keep ahead into the churchyard, bear right, passing in front of the church tower, and go through a kissing gate to return to the start.

Features of Interest

A. With its sleepy air, medieval church, old pub and attractive creamy stone cottages, there is a hint of the nearby Cotswolds at Cleeve Prior. The church – restored in 1863 – dates from the Norman period and its 14th-century tower is a prominent landmark amidst the flat landscape of the vale.

B. The Littletons – North, Middle and South – are a group of small adjacent villages. Middle Littleton has a mainly 13th- and 14th-century church but its most outstanding feature is the huge Tithe Barn, about 140 feet long and 32 feet wide, which belonged to the medieval abbots of Evesham. Documentary evidence indicates that it dates from the late 14th century but its style suggests that it may have been built about a century earlier. The church at South Littleton – passed shortly – has a fine Perpendicular tower and a Norman doorway.

30. Broadway – Tower and Village

Start/Parking: Fish Hill Picnic Place, off A44 at top of Fish Hill – grid reference 120369

Distance: 5½ miles (8.9km)

Category: Moderate

Refreshments: Rookery Barn Restaurant and Café at Broadway Tower Country Park, pubs and cafés at Broadway

Terrain: An easy descent along tracks from the top of the Cotswold escarpment is followed by a stiffer ascent along field paths

OS Maps: Landranger 150, Outdoor Leisure 45

Public transport: Infrequent bus service from Stratford-upon-Avon, Chipping Campden and Moreton-in-Marsh

Explore & Discover

The Cotswolds belong mainly to Gloucestershire and Oxfordshire but a short stretch of the hills runs across the south-eastern corner of Worcestershire above Broadway. From Broadway Tower – which stands on the Cotswold escarpment at the top of Fish Hill – the route descends to Broadway Old Church and continues across fields into the village. A fairly lengthy climb along the Cotswold Way leads back to the start. From the escarpment, the views over the Vale of Evesham are magnificent.

Route Directions

Start by following signs to 'Viewing Point' – there is a viewfinder there but the views are much better further on – and continue beyond it, bearing left and following Cotswold Way signs to the main road. Cross over, take the path opposite, bear right to join a track and almost immediately, bear right again to continue along a winding path through trees to a stile. Climb it, keep ahead to emerge from the woodland and follow the regular Cotswold Way marker posts across the open grassy hilltop towards Broadway Tower. From this point onwards, the views to the right looking across the Vale of Evesham towards the distant line of the

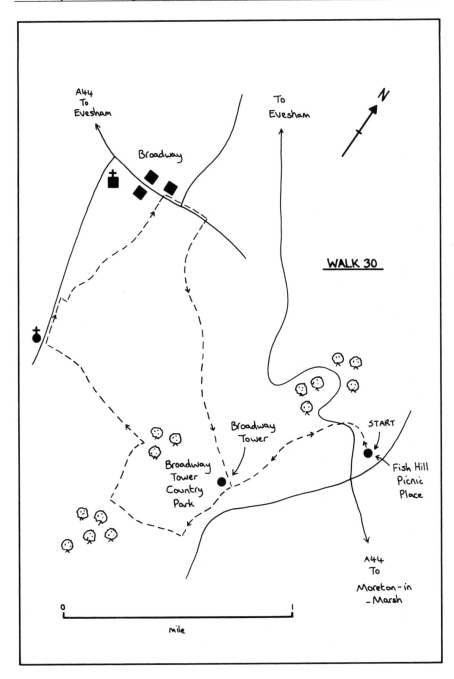

A44
To
Evesham

Broadway

To
Evesham

N

WALK 30

START

Broadway
Tower

Broadway
Tower
Country
Park

Fish Hill
Picnic
Place

A44
To
Moreton-in
-Marsh

0   1

mile

Malverns are superb. After going through two gates you reach the tower. Immediately go through the tall kissing gate ahead to enter Broadway Tower Country Park, [A] keep to the left of the tower, passing a trig point, go through another tall kissing gate and turn right along a tarmac drive that passes to the right of Rookery Barn. In front of gates, bear left onto a path – by a fence on the right – turn right over a ladder stile by a group of beech trees and turn left across a field corner to climb another stile, here leaving the country park.

Turn right onto a downhill tarmac track and where it bends left, bear slightly right to continue along a fence-lined track to a gate. Go through, turn right along a track and after climbing a stile in front of a bungalow, bear left and head downhill across a field to a stile in the bottom left-hand corner. Climb it and walk along a tree-lined track which turns left and continues downhill to emerge onto a road opposite St Eadburgha's Church [B]. Turn right and at a public footpath sign to Broadway, turn right through a kissing gate. Walk along the right field edge, in the corner turn left to continue along the edge and at a fence corner, keep ahead in the same direction across the field to a kissing gate on the far side. Go through, keep ahead across the next field, go through a kissing gate and continue along the left field edge. In the corner go through two kissing gates in quick succession and continue across the next field, making for another kissing gate in a fence corner. Go through that, walk beside an iron fence on the left and continue along an enclosed path into Broadway [C]. The village centre is to the left; the route continues to the right up the main street. After a quarter of a mile (0.4km), turn right, at a Cotswold Way sign, along a track between houses to a stile. Climb it, keep ahead over another and walk across a field, crossing a brook and continuing to a stile on the far side. After climbing that, bear left for the start of the ascent of Fish Hill. Following the regular Cotswold Way marker posts, pass through a hedge gap, bear slightly left to climb a stile, head up to the next marker post and beyond that to another stile in the top right-hand corner of the field. Climb it and continue uphill along the left edge of a series of fields and over a succession of stiles, finally climbing a stile on the edge of the country park. Keep ahead along a fence-lined path to the left of Broadway Tower and turn left through a gate. Here you pick up the outward route and retrace your steps to the start.

Features of Interest

A. Broadway Country Park is based around Broadway Tower, a folly built in 1798 by James Wyatt for the Earl of Coventry. Situated on the Cotswold escarpment at a height of 1024 feet (312m), the views from it are magnificent, looking down on the Vale of Evesham and across to the distant line of the Malverns. In clear conditions the hills of Shropshire and the Black Mountains of South Wales can be seen.

B. The church of St Eadburgha, or Broadway Old Church, about three-quarters of a mile (1.2km) south of the present village, is a most interesting and rewarding building. It has a cruciform plan, with a fine 14th-century central tower, and the interior contains architectural features from the 12th to the 17th centuries. Its 19th-century successor can be seen across the fields to the left on approaching the village.

C. As one of the classic villages of the Cotswolds, Broadway is immensely popular, as its many craft and gift shops, inns and teashops, readily testify and its overall attractiveness has been enhanced by the recent opening of a bypass. Nestling below the Cotswold escarp-

Broadway

ment at the foot of Fish Hill, it developed as a staging post on the main coach route between London and Worcester. The long High Street – the original 'Broad Way – is lined by handsome and distinguished 17th- and 18th-century buildings, all constructed from the local warm-looking limestone, and at the bottom it widens out into a triangular green. In the Victorian era, the village became a fashionable centre for writers and artists, led by William Morris, one of the prominent pre-Raphaelites.

Also of Interest

BEST TEA SHOP WALKS IN WORCESTERSHIRE

Irene Boston

A selection of 25 walks, suitable for all the family, which explore the deeply rewarding landscape of Worcestershire. Centred on towns and villages, the walks explore scenery as diverse as the rolling Malverns, the glorious Wyre Forest, and the northern county canals - all with the promise of a traditional cream tea to follow.   £6.95

GLOUCESTERSHIRE WALKS WITH CHILDREN

Juliet Greenwood

This guide offers variety for all the family - from tranquil woods and meandering river banks to the Gloucester docks. The author hopes the background information and questions which accompany the walks will "stretch the minds of children as well as their legs...and encourage a lifelong love of the countryside".   £6.95

WALKING IN HAUNTED GLOUCESTERSHIRE

Florence Jackson and Gordon Ottewell

Gloucestershire is steeped in ghosts and hauntings, and this is the perfect companion for those who wish to explore the supernatural side of the area, while enjoying excellent walks - "Leaves you waiting for a companion volume" COTSWOLD LIFE.   £6.95

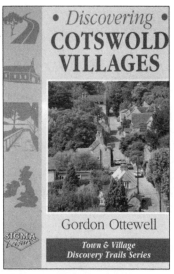

DISCOVERING COTSWOLD VILLAGES
Gordon Ottewell

"Here, in one compact book, is a practical guide for all those who wish to visit - and explore- the most attractive villages in the Cotswolds. Read about the villages, find out about their history, then enjoy one of 50 pleasant walks to uncover the intriguing past of these... settlements".
WORCESTER EVENING NEWS
£6.95

LITERARY STROLLS IN & AROUND THE COTSWOLDS
Gordon Ottewell

A collection of 40 delightful short strolls with special appeal to lovers of literature and landscape.
All less than three miles in length, the routes spread right across the Cotswold countryside and encourage strollers to find out more about the area through the discovery of its many-faceted literary associations. An original approach to walking which will appeal equally to lovers of literature and landscape.
£6.95

All of our books are available through booksellers. In case of difficulty, or for a free catalogue, please contact:
SIGMA LEISURE, 1 SOUTH OAK LANE, WILMSLOW, CHESHIRE SK9 6AR.
Phone: 01625-531035; Fax: 01625-536800.
E-mail: info@sigmapress.co.uk Web site: www.sigmapress.co.uk
MASTERCARD and VISA orders welcome.